D1642535

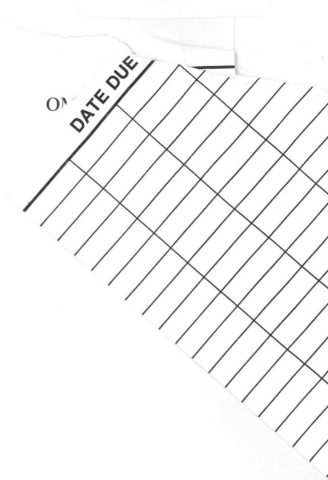

DATE DUE

O

W.N. HERBERT
OMNESIA

(REMIX)

BLOODAXE BOOKS

ISBN: 978 1 85224 969 4 *Omnesia* remix
978 1 85224 962 5 *Omnesia* alternative text

First published 2013 by
Bloodaxe Books Ltd,
Highgreen,
Tarset,
Northumberland NE48 1RP.

www.bloodaxebooks.com
For further information about Bloodaxe titles
please visit our website or write to
the above address for a catalogue.

Supported by
**ARTS COUNCIL
ENGLAND**

Cover design: Neil Astley & Pamela Robertson-Pearce.

Printed in Great Britain by
Bell & Bain Limited, Glasgow, Scotland.

In Memoriam
Maxamed Xaashi Dhamac 'Gaarriye'

(1949-2012)

CONTENTS

PREFACE

Dear reader, I apologise for the position I've put you in. Not just you, but the bookseller, the reviewer, and the various assessors through whose hands one or both aspects of this book has or have had to or will pass or passed – and indeed my publisher, who painstakingly produced two mirror versions of it, one of which you are, probably with increasing reluctance, reading now. And to what end?

Our culture is as happily full of mash-ups, remixes, and directors' cuts, as it is of variorum editions of novelists, poets and playwrights. It is entirely possible in the world of e- (and p-) publishing to imagine any book having several versions, supplemented by additional materials through websites or pamphlets. So, I wondered, why not write a book which absorbs that flexibility into its basic structure?

Hence *Omnesia*, a book in two volumes and neither, its title both a portmanteau and a sort of oxymoron, pairing 'omniscience' ('You must know everything') with 'amnesia', an often traumatic condition of forgetfulness. For me, writing a book of poetry is both of these, simultaneously a shoring up and a letting go. (In fact, for me, being in the world is also like this – perhaps that's why so much of this book is on the move, between tones and genres as much as places, not quite at home in any of them.)

So writing a book of poetry becomes both punk experiment and prog system. That is, I go with the emphatic flow of its inspirations, I forget everything a poem 'should' be, and improvise its subjects, its themes, its forms and tones, but at the same time I am constantly trying to orchestrate these into a whole, thinking of them as sections that contrast, complement and speak to each other.

This echoes my reading experience, in which any book that has moved, troubled or changed me begins to exist as one version in my head, and another in my hand. To the extent to which it has such an effect, it becomes 'my' book, and begins to be imagined as a collaboration between myself and the author, or by a sort of third mind that knows what we both know. Then, when I re-read the actual book, I find there is so much I have forgotten, or overlooked, or mistaken, that it has become yet another book. These two versions then enter into further dialogue.

While I was writing *Omnesia* – or rather while I was lying on a bed daydreaming before an event at the Cuírt Festival in Galway – I began to wonder if these various dynamics could be embodied in two physically distinct but twin-like books.

In my first Bloodaxe volume, *Forked Tongue*, I had suggested the principle of 'And not Or' to position a poetic of variousness in a market that favours (if not fetishises) concision and restraint. All my books since have been doubled – linguistically, stylistically or thematically. *Omnesia* takes that principle one step further: the various sections in each volume mirror, juxtapose, continue or contrast. Hopefully, they make one sense read in isolation, and a further read together.

What this interrelation does not appear to be is a dialectic – it is not that debate between thesis and antithesis which our media loves, creating pantomime oppositions in order to pitch common sense against complexity. It's more like the dance between ideas we encounter in the ancient mode of strophe and antistrophe, each step taking the step it echoes and reflecting it onto another level: the epode arises from this, not as a matter of logical synthesis, but as news from nowhere.

Of course, you needn't concern yourself with this unless it engages you: this volume can be read by itself, and only if you are at all moved, troubled or changed need it be considered in conjunction with its non-identical twin. I hope you are (moved, troubled or changed), not least because it will double my sales, a consideration I should confess occurred to me almost immediately after the principles outlined above.

Even the forgetting of something, in which every relationship of being towards what one formerly knew has been obliterated, must be viewed as a *modification of the primordial being-in*; and this holds for every delusion and for every error.

HEIDEGGER

I think you don't believe half the lies I'm telling you.

WILLIE CLANCY

Scallop

The first shell's half sat on sand-coloured tiles,
my grandparents' fireplace surround,
receiving the squat stubs' grind, doups of decades
of Granda's failing puff – a stand-in, really,
for that globe on a chrome stilt,
like Ost Berlin's communications tower,
Corso Street's own Telespargal:
a top button sliced open its steel floor
from which ciggies tumbled like failed Bond villains
to an oubliette of ash.
                              Its successors
washed up years later on a seventies' tide
in throwback restaurants, or spun toward us
like shuriken saucers in teppanyaki bars,
each bearing the browned-off stump
of a former inhabitant or her neighbour –
wee Aphrodites of Loch Fyne,
giant extracted pencil erasers of Fraserburgh,
nipples of queenies, thumb-flesh of kings.
In the mouth they were soft fibre, nut butter,
like the engorged gills of oyster mushrooms.

The last time I stared at their fluted spaulders
was on a little chapeled island where
experts prised open coffins' shells
on the little skeletons of pilgrims –
medieval Lucies, eyeless hominids, hobbit-Catholics,
peregrines caught mid-flight from Finisterre,
their holy route now shielded from our feet, our eyes
by history's nacre, that slug-slow translator
of mendicant and seeker – whatever they savoured,
no matter their sins or skills – into drifters, tourists.

And on every sternum like an emblem
as if grafted by a byssus onto bone, that fossil wing,
fanned hands-width shelter for each soul's nub: a scallop.

1 EL SUR

I have transformed into another
and the role is going well for me
and the landscapes?
I see inside maps of flesh with my bat eyelids...
softened over a stake
I see sown fields of paper in ossuaries
I have turned my suit inside out to cover appearances
I wear a mask
I have been another

JUAN CALZADILLA,
tr. Katharine Hedeen & Víctor Rodríguez Núñez

Mount Avila

Time to be climbing out of time
as the wild city rates it, receding from
the cable car rising from Caracas
into the marriage of leaf and mist:
a great ship composed of greying droplets
is docking at the summit of Avila
and Argelia and I must get there before
its rain-crew disembark and birdsong
resiles into its respective throats.

But first the child in a Cuban forage cap
must cry '*no amo caer*' and her mother
must laugh, whether we fall or not,
and each tree beneath our swaying feet
must fill a bell-tower built from fog
with its shaking carillon of hangdog leaves
which dream of becoming second-hand books
laid on the pavement in the Parque Central:
Idiot's Guide to World Poetry, La Prisión de la Imaginación.

We leap from the cradle and into the haze,
pass among the sellers of *arepas* and *melocotón*
along the path stretched like a sagging clothesline
between the sweating cold palms of the fog
past the dogs that guard these heights
from the piratical stars, the thieving galaxies.
We pass by the blind dejected telescopes
and approach the colossal, mostly-obscured,
mist-broken column of the Humboldt Hotel.

It's only as we stand beneath the topless trees
pissing down their panicking legs, waiting for
the piano bar to open, that I realise
an invisible horse has been following me
for some time – translucent notes
hanging from its eyelashes betray

its presence, truculent and shy as always,
summoned by *helados* and bullets wrapped
in handkerchieves, on the thighs of mangoes.

And it's only as the mist clears and unclears
like a sea rendering up its depths, its dead,
its patient staring inhabitants,
and the horse and Argelia and I drink beer
in the English Bar, even though we're so cold
and the bar is not even sub-mock-Tudor,
that I understand the world is the wrong way up,
that mountaintops protrude down into Lethe
and that we are in the grip of a devilfish.

As if to confirm this conclusion a host of devilbirds
flash their unknown yellow tails in Vs
and display the nerve-coloured blue of their breasts
and begin to converse in a cluttering language
only sailors of these dimensions could have devised
to be understood by those beings eager
to pass among the stars without questions.
Of course it is already dark as a horse
and we look down upon the city giving birth to hours.

La Cabeza de Ternero

Why did I buy you, tender-eyed decapitated head of a calf
or rather skin of the calf, hornless and delicate of ear,
like the hovering wings of a bat, pinkish with the sunset behind,
brown short-haired caramel skin stretched over a wooden skull
and set with glass marbles made tender by their setting

in the artisans' market of the Guajiro people beside the burnt-out
grey concrete mass of the Hotel Bahia like a legionnaires' fort
abandoned in the desert, before it a well-pierced San Sebastian
for this was Maracaibo where the lake is like an eye
with a second eye beneath it, socket filled with oil,
where Chavez finds displeasing graffiti on the walls
and responds, so that across the road a municipal block
has the legend running along its uppermost storey
PATRIA, SOCIALISMO O MUERTE, with the allegory
'Distribuye alimentos derrotando el acaparamiento'?

Was it because of the boy dressed as Bolivar in the community centre
who brandished both a cutlass and a poem about the birth of Venezuela?
Or the stilt-walker with whitewashed features who smiled so freely
outside in the melting dusk? Was it because of the laundrywoman
who found the face of an icon in the foam and soapsuds?

Or was it because of the bust parked unheroically on a brick wall
in the blocks they're demolishing for El Paseo de la Ciencias,
for more greenery like the extra layers of ribbons generals receive,
and to house the fibre-glass colonnade which contains
the giant Virgin of Chiquinquirá whose image was found
floating on a small board in Lake Maracaibo among the laundry?
Or the many balloons of Mickey Mouses hanging outside
the tiny shops across from the bright blue Santa Barbara,
each pediment and arch picked out in snow cloud like
the innumerable eyebrows of an exasperated Zulian sky-god.

Was it the veal, the beef, the shame of eating butchered meat?
The pork, the poultry, game; the guilt inside jaw's joy?
The hock and haunch, the tail and wing, the shoulder, rib;
leaving only your hollowed head of hide? Was it the hunger
for guilt at what we visit on that which is not our own?

Was it because we pulled up beside one of Maracaibo's
narrow-fronted, two-storeyed, elaborately stuccoed,
powder-sky-blue buildings, with some saint's institution
picked out on the front, and round the corner was
the smooth curve of a deco-block in a decaying gravy hue,
as though these were the brow and flank of livestock?
Or the long wreck of a low-slung Chevy which pulled up
beside us, its winged tail-lights round white sockets, its trunk
and back seat hollowed out into a single broad metal groove,
its hood a noble bashed-in-and-out-again half-repainted skull?

Was it because my breakfast croissant looked like the head of a *conejo*?
Was it because of the butterflies taxiing up and down the runways
at the *aeropuerto*? Was it because of the Virgin floating to the shore
on a washing board and the laundrywoman who looked into her face
and saw the clean and tender eyes of a slaughtered calf?

Distribuye alimentos derrotando el acaparamiento: distributing food defeating
hoarding.

Cojedes County

Caballo viejo no puede
perder la flor que le dan
porque después de esta vida
no hay otra oportunidad

EL CABALLO VIEJO

1

From a bottled bear and an old grey horse –
the *autopista*'s growl and the llanos' song;
from a mango tree and a branch of *mamón*,
Cojedes makes a *cuatro*, I make this verse.

Cowboy harp on the taxi radio
hectic and haptic, the opposite of mist:
white butterflies clouding the *cayenas* –
red hibiscus for *El Caballo Viejo*.
The grey horse song takes us down the road
past the Polar plant's logo, a beer-bear;
the truckstop out of *Terminator* –
all bashed steel counters, hot scratched glass,
cheap cuatros hanging in dusty plastic;
then autopista for a few hours more.

Holy cornbread, sweet and brittle,
bought from the narrowing road's hot sides
as we enter Cojedes State – poor trade
sunk in trees, and through them, fat cattle.
Branches balled with bubblegum fruit that'll
stain everything if dripped: tooth the rind,
release the *mamón*'s goo, don't mind
the mess: we're at the giant mango,
the plastic fruit that marks San Carlos,
punning the moon in an cartoon sky.

20

2

From a streetful of dancers and a cross of flowers –
guarapita and *cinco de mayo*;
from buckets of steak, and beers by the crate-load:
Cojedes makes a *cuatro*, I make this verse.

Bolas Criollas before the night reading
with *el Papa de los Helados*' crew
in the veterans' club: packed dirt, hard looks;
then down to the river: a weaving
of orchids with words but, preceding
that, two old *gatos*, with their backs to us,
speed-strummed to *la Madre*, sang to the cross
and summoned up drums – a wave-crest
from darkness, a foaming of dresses,
dances where poetry should be lost.

Guarapita's kick, *el Papa*'s '*¡Na' guará!*' –
the night can't know it's become a cartoon
where Herriman sketches that mango moon,
old horses drink to forget their tomorrows
and glass bears clink to their icy marrows.
Tomorrow I'll buy a four-stringed guitar
I can't play; now, we sing to the stars
melodies echoed by a sizzle of sirloins:
es mejor beberse el día que vivirlo –
and crazy as *el caballo*, I make this verse.

el Papa de los Helados: the Pope of Icecreams.
¡Na' guará!: wow!
Es mejor beberse el día que vivirlo: it's better to drink the day away than live.

The Morlocks

When we were thirteen we knew we'd live forever,
Mojo, Marshall, Mike and Me: eternally Morlock.
Thirty years later we'd only always been around.
By then Marshall had sued us for all the money
we now must watch decay into the future.

The grey wigs gave way to grey hairs then
to wigs again; our elder brothers' leathers, nicked
and spray-painted as silverbacks, were replaced
by bombers embossed with the Moscow Metro's
haloed M (once we'd settled out of court).

Our favourite/only four chords became four phases
of fail: shed-rock schlock and sunk-punkadelica,
retardo-prog soufflé and grungewagon breakdown.
We always meant to be the undergroundest hogs,
sous les chats froids, beneath the earth-pig, sub-mole –

we just thought immortality would come attached.
The concept was clear as time-travel to a plumber:
all our gigs to be played in basements or caves,
the songs to be three minutes short: 'Morticia',
'I Ate Rod Taylor's Mam', 'Moonburn My Arse'.

So there were follies: cutting all Marshall's solos,
then releasing them as sawn-off instrumentals
on 'Jellied Eloi'; the M-shaped tour of Morocco
where M was for muggings; the Fresh Pit Festival
and its JCB logistics. But we had triumphs if not hits –

Joan Collins reprising the role of Nellifer for
the 'Love in the Mausoleum' vid; 'Myetro to Moscow',
bootlegged in OGI, our best ever gig – although
'Underground Sunrise in Elektrozavodskaya'
was a synth too far – we lost our Mojo. That US tour,

when the Yank Morlocks' lawyers wouldn't let us
use the name, so we cranked up bouzoukis
and called ourselves The Malakas – they loved it,
although Mike fell in the Mississippi, caught
St Louis encephalitis, and had to be retired.

I may have gone out on one of Limbo's outer limbs
with the concept album, but sales in Japan
for 'Apocalyptic Rabbit Is Our Friend'
were better than the record label claimed
when it dropped us – and it isn't true,

as Marshall's replacement Marlene 'revealed',
that my rider included a kilo of carrot
grated into a litre of vodka, or that the crew
peed a fresh pentagram on stage each night.
And no, Mojo didn't have a sex change and rejoin.

People often ask if I could travel back in time
what would I tell the band? A quarter of nothing
is still fuck all, Marshall. Mojo, I'll sell the Moog
when you sell the microwave. Mike, once a Morlock
always a Morlock: call me. Me? Don't smoke crack.

Pilgrim Street

_having felt... that between us a vague but immediate relationship
had established itself, an undefined but real rapport, an inexplicable
but undeniable communication, I have tried to portray in music
a few of my strongest sensations and most lively impressions._

LISZT on 'Les Années de Pelerinage'

1 *Chield*

My voice went on a quest to find itself –
it never breathed a word to me about
its divvy divagations. On the shelf
I fashioned fonts from flies, their snorkel pouts
for punctuation, trumpet crossed with trout.
Meanwhile, its palate for a scallop, off
my voice went down to Pilgrim Street, to shouts
of dry support from beetles, left one cough
to build a colophon: my capitals
were spiders and my type trepanned through ancient skulls.

Hit that bone ceiling and both past and future
glaze over, right and wrong brick up, the floor's
a stairwell with no spine. So Jung's computer,
which consciousness can access with a snore,
hovered in darkness like a bat indoors,
mute, while, monkey-mouthed, my voice immersed
itself in others' words like lakes; explored
each continent in haste for signs of verse;
sought out new Helicons of alcohol,
new mountains for old muses and new ways to fall.

So for these last few years (let's call it seven,
since numbers please compulsives and the page),
I've been invited on my travels; even,
(let's talk it up) to make Geek Pilgrimage.
A very passive knight, I must engage
with other peoples and their poetries;

must leave my house and, almost, act my age –
that's me, for whom 'outside' is a disease,
whose verse is manga made iconostasis,
obliged to learn, to taste and visit actual places.

Of course (I know this now the ship has sailed),
the whole clan was nomadic way back when –
before we built our boat of fools, fools trailed
from Africa – plus proto-Herbert men.
Yes, long before the reed became the pen
we all went walk-n-wadeabout who crossed
to Yemen when the Red Sea was a fen,
spread from Djibouti to points north. We lost
some melanin like luggage in the Ice Age,
then claimed we were sole authors of the human message.

We feel the same about our prosody
today and, whether we must innovate
linguistically or craft our monodies
on Morgan or Donaghy, we think we're GRRREAT...
Forgive me if I drift from that debate
back to my sad *otaku* quest: the game
of justifying what my instincts state:
the Silk Road and the Low Road are the same.
(In Japanese *shūgyō* means errantry –
while here it means that Shug disputes yir parentry.)

The Low Road and the Silk Road are the same:
you needn't know yourself to cross the globe,
and no cartography's required to dream,
but still, the Gobi's twinned with frontal lobes –
your neurons are oases; myelin robes
protect their merchandise of messages –
neuroses must be sold to allophobes,
philosophies spice up *la grande sagesse*.
My ancestors, though never so far east,
were travellers, twisters, tinks, skeletal at thought's feast.

The Herberts tend to yield sarcastic chields:
travelling showmen, shooting gallery
and shoggie-boat proprietors – from fields
of dupes drop to a lorry driver's salary –
unhappy scrappies, stickit merchants, at sea
in sober streets; quixotic engineers,
faith-loupers, seekers of higher calories;
genealogists of the tricky years,
brickies not thickies, dyers not liars: the cream
of chicken soup of those found drowning in their dreams.

Otaku: (Japanese) obsessive, geek.

2 THE DAFTNESS

Yir heid's daft, yir belly's saft,
and yir bum is medd o leather...

ANCIENT DUNDONIAN SAYING

Rabbie, Rabbie, Burning Bright

Atween November's end and noo
there's really nithin else tae do
but climb inside a brindlet coo
      and dream o Spring,
fur Winter's decked hur breist and broo
      wi icy bling.

It feels like, oan St Andrae's nicht,
thi sun went oot and gote sae ticht
he endit up in a braw fire fecht
      wi some wee comet –
noo he's layin low wi his punched-oot licht
      aa rimmed wi vomit.

We too hae strachilt lik The Bruce
and hacked up turkey, duck and goose;
and let aa resolution loose
      oan Hogmanay,
but waddle noo frae wark tae hoose
      lyk dogs they spayed.

Each year fails tae begin thi same:
fae dregs o Daft Deys debt comes hame
and we gaither in depression's wame
      aa duty-crossed –
but Burns's birthday is a flame
      set tae Defrost.

Ye dinna need tae be Confucius
tae ken, if Dullness wad confuse us,
ye caa 'Respite! Let's aa get stocious –
      And dinna nag us.
Grant us that globe of spice, thi luscious
      Delight caaed "haggis"!'

That truffle o the North must be
dug frae the depths o January,
but cannae pass oor lips, nor we
        cross Limbo's border –
unless that passport, Poetry,
        be quite in order.

Sae thi daurkest deys o thi haill damn year
can dawn in yawns baith dreich an drear –
sae thi Taxman's axe is at wir ear
        fur his Returns?
We Scots sall neither dreid nor fear
        but read wir Burns.

Atween: between; strachilt: struggled; wark: work; stocious: inebriated; dreich:
miserable.

An Epistle

Leeze me on rhyme! It's ay a treasure,
My chief, amaist my only pleasure
BURNS

While London's steekit beh thi snaw
and ilka sleekit chitterin jaw
     is ettlin tae describe
hoo drifts ur white, and ice is cauld,
and feel thi lave maun be enthralled –
       Eh've Bowmore tae imbibe.
And as the nicht – mair dreh nor me –
   draas in, Eh think Eh'll scrieve
a wee epistle tae, let's see,
    thi deid and Doctor Grieve –
       auld hermits, wee MacDiarmids,
         thi ghaist o guid Lapraik:
        here's a ravie fur young Davie,
         an a rant fur Rabbie's sake.

For the tartan telephone is playin
'Fur Auld Lang Syne'; some cloud's displayin –
well, it's no quite the Batsign – weans
     wull hae nae clue,
but aa thir dominies are prayin
     tae Burns's Ploo.

Some anniversary or ither
huz gote thi lot tae plot thigither
and ask frae whaur – Stranraer? – or whither
     remeid sall come:
they've caaed aa gowks fur blinks o blether
     baith deep and dumb.

32

In stately manses Haggismen
puhl sheeps' wames owre thir heids and then
descend beh greenie poles tae dens
          whaur desks await;
they raise thir stumpy Haggispens
          and smear on slates.

While maskless weemen keep ut edgy
an gee wir man a retro-wedgie –
remind us hoo his views got sketchy
          on burds and...beasts;
demand thir haggises be veggie
          and, glorious, feast.

And aa the waant-tae-bes are Robins
mair willin tae wark hard than Dobbin
and fuhl o antifreeze fae bobbin
          fur bacon rinds –
thir beaks, aa chipped, let slip thi sobbin
          of achin minds.

Thi anely time that Scots gets read
is when thi year lukes nearly dead –
          it seems tae need extremes;
when winterin leaves are lipped wi frost
and wolf-pack winds pursue the lost
          and ink, in deep freeze, dreams.
When Naichur jinks yir toon's defence
     and bursts yir comfort's net
wi snaw fitbaas, then tae thi tense
     come wurds thi waurm furget:
          deep-layerin, like swearin,
               we dig oot attitudes;
          wi stanzas come answers
               tae city pseuds and prudes.

33

Whit Burns wiz sayin tae Lapraik
wiz whit we are's eneuch tae make
a puckle lines that salve life's paiks:
          we need nae ticks
nor teachers' nods, nor critics' shakes –
          we're no that thick.

Ut's no that anely crambo goes
that jingles oot, jejunely, woes:
Burns claims he disnae ken whit's prose,
          whit's poetry,
but see hoo crafty his rhyme flows,
          and braid as Tay.

Whit Burns bethankit Davie fur
wiz freenship in thi dargin dirr:
when, pure ramfeezelt, thochts gae whirr,
          tae knock back gills
by ithers' ingles, bields fae smirr,
          can stave aff ills.

But here Eh sit wi midnicht's nip,
or leh doon whaur thi verses slip,
or rise tae brose and habbies' grip
          aa oan ma tod,
neglectin meh professorship,
          in the nemm o Gode!

Fur twenty fehv years – mair – Eh've trehd
tae scrieve in Scots and it's nae leh
that billy's gone – sae why deneh
          Eh've ootlived Burns?
Fae Davie tae Lapraik we fleh
          wi nae returns.

Ootlived, but no ootwritten yet,
nae superbard, nor Guardian pet
        nor whit maist fowk wad read;
tho fit fur (no sae) prehvut letters
wi a dictionair sae crossword-setters
        micht love me when Eh'm deid.
But whit Burns foond inben oor speak's
    a glede fur aa McSlackers:
gin Doric's heat is kin tae Greek
    Eh'll scrieve 'To a Moussaka.'
        And thi ithers? Jist brithers
        and sisters eftir aa:
        still-hopefu peers and hoped-fur feres –
        Eh think thi ink micht thaw...

Steekit: forced shut; *chitterin:* chattering with cold; *ettlin:* attempting; *the lave:*
the rest, the hoi polloi; *maun:* must; *scrieve:* write; *dominies:* teachers; *ploo:* plough;
remeid: remedy; *puhl:* pull; *eneuch:* enough; *a puckle:* a few; *pains:* blows; *crambo:*
verse, doggerel; *dargin dirr:* exhaustion of physical labour; *ramfeezelt:* exhausted
to the point of confusion; *bields:* shelters; *smirr:* fine rain; *billy:* young lad; *deneh:*
deny; *inben:* within; *glede:* flame; *feres:* comrades.

To a Moussaka

Moussaka, multistorey prince
of scoff – furst aubergine then mince
then tatties tappit wi a chintz
     o bechamel –
ye gift fae Greeks that brings on grins
     jist beh yir smell.

Pagoda o thi denner table,
as tooers gae, an anti-Babel,
ye mak the universe feel stable –
     wan tongue wull pass
fur taste and toast: let aa wha's able
     creh oot '*Yia mas!*'

Some noodles claim *Pastitsio*'d
win ony prehz – no in this ode;
nor *Kleftiko* can steal thi vote
     nor *Soutzoukakia*:
let them that miss oor dish's boat
     wear *Papoutsakia*.

There's some prefer ye cut fae trays,
some baked in pottingers o clay,
some add courgettes and some say nay –
     but aa agree
thi furst true taste o Holiday
     can anely be...

Moussáka! – said as amphibrach
tho that micht mak a Cretan lauch:
it shid be cretic here, but, ach,
     whit's *Moússakás*?
Ah'm fae Dundee, sae in meh sprach,
     nae use at aa!

But Eh've plenty o rhymes fur a guid *Moussaka*
far mair nor Greece huz financial backers –
did Clytemnestra, husband-whacker
  hae as mony whacks?
Constantinople rank attackers
  lyk this at thi Sack?

– as mony as forks besiegin *Moussakas*
wieldit beh genius or beh jackass,
Kazantzakhes or some *vlakas*
  aa shiftin amoonts –
ye'd need an abacus (or jist Bacchus)
  tae haundle thi coont.

Sae be an archaeologist
o appetite, dig thru its crust
and nose thi *nostimáda* – mist
  o history;
this Byzantine wee treisure kist
  that aa can pree.

Thi Padishah wad dine on this,
thi Doge gee his lasagne a miss,
thi Emperor bestow a kiss
  upon uts cook:
its pages spell a book o bliss,
  come tak a look –

or tak a moothfu, rich and reamin –
then sing, ye weel-contentit weemen,
since Eh, fou-stappit, faa tae dreamin;
  sing oot, ye masters:
hud Troy a horse filled wi this daimon,
  it'd faan faur faster!

Tappit: topped; *beh:* by; *yia mas!:* (Greek) to us!; *prehz:* prize; *vlakas:* (Greek)
blockhead; *nostimáda:* (Greek) tastiness; *reamin:* smooth, overflowing.

Lines on the New Makar

(for Liz Lochhead)

Ye citizens upon thi Broo
and evrywan thi Tories screw
while bankers aa thir sins renew,
      jine me, rejoice!
Fur Liz wull be oor Makar noo:
      we hae a voice.

See Scotland's three furst meenisters,
a bunch o bawheids, ye may curse,
thank Christ they seem tae ken thir verse –
      they've made thir choice;
let England snib its mim-moud purse,
      we hae a voice.

Parliaments think they'll aye be heard
but cannae ootlive a makar's wurd:
in Liz they've met a gallus bard –
      wi grace an poise
she'll bind us aa intae wan chord:
      we hae a voice.

Gode kens the moontaintaps are deef,
The depths o lochs haud nae beliefs,
There is nae border tae oor griefs,
      But still, rejoice:
Ae singer is the hert's relief,
      we hae a voice.

Thi Broo: unemployment benefit; *bawheids:* fatheads; *ken:* know; *snib:* click shut;
mim-moud: affectedly proper; *gallus:* lively, forceful; *ae:* one, only one.

38

Bawheid

1

Pollin, pollin, pollin
tho Labour heids are rollin
keep them Tories groanin
Bawheid!
Hydro, ile and whisky
wull keep oor kintry frisky
when we are free frae Tory greed
aa thi joys we're missin –
sane policies fur fishin –
are things that ivry bawheid huz agreed.

(Bawheid won thi protest vote
that waants oor boat o gowks tae float
but thinks its hull an unca notion –
he says he'll sort thon oot mid-ocean...)
Vote him in, big him up
bugger them, vote them oot
shove him in, hoy them oot,
Bawheid!

Keep votin, votin, votin,
tho dreamin o Kropotkin
keep them Tories gropin,
Bawheid!
they dinnae treh tae understand us,
jist bully-rule and brand us –
soon we'll be free o Tory greed
noo Braveheart's calculatin
hoo tourists wull be savin
tae visit thi shrine o Jimmy Reid.

(Bawheid disnae rock thi boat
while Libdems queue tae act thi goat
and Labour's pishin on its waa
he needna gang tae sea at aa...)

Get them oot, slide him in –
bidies-in, stoppers-oot:
shut them oot, lock him in,
Bawheid!

2

Bawheid pleys thi EveryJock
that craws his kintry huz been twocked –
in ilka parish bawheids spawn
lyk puddocks wi a toorie on:

This bawheid's fiss is vast and flat,
thon bawheid's lugs are miles apart;
this bawheid's skull is fuhl o mince –
he thocht thi wance but huznae since...

Ane bawheid loups thi fitbaw fence
tae show a Tim hoo fists mak sense
o Scotland's auld dichotomies –
whit need o teams wi fans lyk these?

This bawheid's mooth is fuhl o teeth
lyk tombstanes nicked fae Cowdenbeath,
thon bawheid's een ur stirkie's baas
thru which he niver looks at aa.

Anither asks wi trippin pus
'Whit huv thi English din fur us?'
Yir bawheid maks a braw contrarian
altho he's niver heard o Darien...

1. *Ile:* oil; *gowks:* fools; *unca:* unusual, unlikely; *bidies-in, stoppers-oot:* those who
won't go out, and those who won't go home.
2. *Craws:* crows; *puddocks:* frogs; *toorie:* a worsted knob on a bonnet; *fiss:* face;
lugs: ears; *loups:* leaps; *a Tim:* abusive term for a Catholic; *stirkie:* steer; *pus:* face.

Carpe Darien

Nae king there sat in Holyrood
nae corn stude in the field
but the Company of Scotland swore
tae find the nation bield.

'O wha will sail oor bonny ships
and whaur sall they be sent?'
'Sir William Paterson's the man
tae find us Darien.'

And ilka carle and ilka laird
hes foond a coin or mair,
and sent it tae Sir William
and ilk sall hae a share.

'Tae Darien, tae Darien,
tae stitch the East tae West.'
There wiz nae Scotsman tae be foond
wha'd jouk the pilgrim's test.

Five ships upon the Munonday
set sail frae sonsy Leith
tae set fit on the New World's green
and daur the Spaniard's teeth.

Twal hunnert men and weemen were
oor Adams and oor Eves
that bigged a hame in Paradise
weel-boddened by thir nieves.

They hudna been a month, a month
in Panama but twae
when that the Spanish captains aa
did offer them tae slay.

'Mak ready, mak ready,' Sir William cried,
'They sall not roond the Bay,
for we hae fifty cannon primed
tae send them on thir way.'

They hadna been a year, a year
when Pestilence arrived
and tuke the young, the hale, the auld,
and tuke Sir William's wife.

'I saw the new mune late yestreen
wi the auld mune in her airm:
I fear the New World claims my banes
and sune maun hap ma bairn.'

'O whaur will I get a guid sailor
tae speel the watchtooer stair
and spy oot when doth come remeid
for we are near despair.'

'O here am I, a sailor guid
tae speel the watchtooer stair,
but I fear the English king's blockade
sall mean there's nae ship there.'

He hadna tane a step, a step
when they heard a lude hurray
and saw the Dolphin, panged wi spiles,
come sailin roond the Bay.

O blithely blithely ran they doon
tae keek intae the hold:
nae silks they saw but sacks o wheat
and saut beef guid as gold.

'We foond an English trader bark
aa boond for Port Royal,
and prentit banknotes frae thir sails
wi Scottish cannonballs.'

'And lang the Governor will sit
and fan him wi his hat
while we dine on his Lordship's hams
and Demarara vat.'

Sir William laid his wife and bairn
fu meekly in the mould
and twined a lock frae ilkane's hair
and said, 'Noo I am auld.'

'But simmer's heat at last is past
and we hae breid eneuch,
nor England's ban nor Spanish hand
sall cast us from this cleuch!'

And aa that Company o Scots
gaithered roond him then
the livin and the deid aneath
the sile o Darien.

Fair fa, fair fa, tae Panama,
the font o oor remeid,
whaur ilka coin o Scottish gowd
wiz paid fur by oor deid.

Find bield: make safe or secure; *jouk:* dodge; *sonsy:* thriving; *daur:* dare; *bigged:*
built; *weel-boddened:* well-prepared or furnished; *nieves:* fists; *yestreen:* last night;
hap: cover; *speel:* climb; *panged:* crammed; *keek:* look; *saut:* salt; *ilkane:* each
one; *cleuch:* cliff.

43

The Daftness

Thi Daftness maks thi truth suppose
it comes in whaur thi fable goes,
gets poetry tae luke at prose
        as tho they're sib,
thi scriever tae luke doon'iz nose,
        'That's *Mister* Nibs.'

Thi Daftness sits up in thi dark
and hears thi siller birkies bark,
in aa thi dullness it's thi spark
        reveals thi scene;
it swaps thi houlet fur thi lark
        since aa's a dream.

Thi Daftness turns us heelstergowdie,
swaps thi baukie fur thi mowdie,
maks thi presbyter a rowdy,
        it birls us roond
till Chanticleer becomes Howtowdie –
        nae dawn? Nae soond.

Thi Daftness flips oor love-life owre
and causes cocky cunts tae cower
while losers in thir wee sma hours
        unlock thi knees
o thae wha itherwise wad lour
        on keys lyk these.

Thi Daftness turns oor history
back upstream fae thi thankless sea
tae bens o possibility
        and glens o smoke:
Flodden unlost, thi Union a lee,
        John Knox a joke.

(Thi Daftness disnae actually
dae ony o thi things Eh say –
thon wid be daft – it's Scotland's play
     at Saturnalia:
luked at lyk this there is no way
     we're aa jist failures.)

Sib: kindred; *siller birkies:* silver birches; *houlet:* owl; *heelstergowdie:* head over heels; *baukie:* bat; *mowdie:* mole; *birls:* whirls, spins; *Howtowdie:* a hen that has never laid, an unmarried woman; *lour:* glare.

A Myth of Scotland

Even twenty years ago, given the large proportion of the population descended from successive waves of settlers, the teaching of Scottish history and literature was a commonplace in South America and in the southern United States. However, Scottish Studies have fallen into a sudden and appalling state of decay since the final collapse of the Second Republic in 1998, exactly three hundred years after the establishment of New Caledonia in Panama. I therefore intersperse a few comments to contextualise this brief selection of poems.

The astonishing rapid success of the Darien Scheme, which meant settlers had driven the Caledonian Canal through that narrow isthmus of land between the two oceans by 1707, ensured that Scotland had won at least mercantile independence, and could begin to plot secession from the more material dominion of the English.

By 1796, then, and the establishing of the first Scots Republic, the wealth of South American trade had transformed the nation's capital, and herds of llamas roamed the Highlands. The literary scene, too, was thriving, as a wealthy Edinburgh supported the renewed interest in the Scots 'language' as it was reclassified, and the craze for 'Ploughman Poets' meant that more successful figures like Robert Burns could retire from physical labour and hold literary court, drawing the nascent English 'Romantics' north.

FROM *To a Llama*

O humpless camel, eel-neckit sheep,
brocht tae Scotia owre the Deep
fae Darien tae nibble neeps,
      maist haughty Llama,
fae Panama tae Perth, ye leap
      oor panorama.

Yet when I glance intae yir een
nae insicht in there dae I glean
at aa thae views ye maun hae seen
    Peebles tae Peru!
Yir gove is dozent, lunkit, mean,
    ye parvenu.

Ye mind me o thae English bardies
wha hunker roond me in thir cardies
nithert, noddin, Ned-come-tardies
    that luke sae glum –
De Quincy, Keats – aa dull Worthwardies
    oan laudanum...

Gove: vacant stare; *dozent:* spiritless; *lunkit:* lukewarm; *nithert:* trembling with cold.

Throughout the 19th century, Scottish writing thrived, with Scott's invention of detective fiction in *The Murder of Midlothian*, a re-creation of the assassination of Bonny Prince Charlie, or 'BPC' as he became known. Hogg's *Confessions of a Justified Winner* satirised the dubious morality of the Scottish entrepreneur, whose wealth was gained not just in Central America and the West Indies, but on the slave plantations of the southern states of the US. When the Dundee poet William MacGonagall visited New York in 1887, Scottish writers were still held in sufficient esteem that he was immediately introduced to Walt Whitman, with whom he formed a long and affectionate friendship.

FROM *The Queen of New Jersey*

When I first came to the Town of New York
I bobbed up Broadway like a cork
and happened upon a lecture by the Good Grey Poet,
Walt Whitman of Camden, and before you could know it
I became his best friend because of my rhymes
which he thought as rough as my hands or the times

and said that my hair was as dark as Poe's raven
and that he liked a Scotchman to be clean-shaven
whereas his beard and hair was as white as Glencoe
and he was away to eat shad in Gloucester, and would I like to go?
And soon we shared his cottage in Camden
and I was as happy as a Rangers fan in Hampden...

By the early twentieth century, Scotland's 'empire' was taking on
an increasingly virtual existence, while the advocacy of 'Scots' as a
separate language began to seem increasingly anachronistic. Small
wonder that a new and iconoclastic school of poets arose in response
to Scotland's neutrality during the First World War, advancing
realpolitik theories of Union with England, and satirising the trad-
itionalists. The most prominent of these was Christopher Murray
Grieve, who invented the comic persona of 'Hugh MacDiarmid',
most baroque of Scotsmen.

The Gutterjaw

Ae dreich forenoon whaur the spew's whummelt
Eh heard thon gantin soon
a gutterjaw wi'iz harns kicked oot
address thi mune –
and Eh thocht o the wey yir fiss luked torn
when you were born.

Eh didnae keek in thi chanty's bowl that nicht,
Eh hudnae time,
but Eh hae thocht o thon pissheid's speak
ever sin syne –
and Eh think ilka nicht as Eh pit ye tae bed
ye'll growe up a ned.

Gutterjaw: one who expresses himself in the speech of the gutter; *whummelt:*
spilled; *gantin:* slack-jawed; *harns:* brains; *fiss luked torn:* had an upset expression;
chanty: chamber pot; *ned:* aggressive person.

Grieve's cynical vision of intra-British politics appeared justified by Churchill's decision to occupy Scotland during World War Two in order to prevent England being surrounded by questionably 'neutral' states. The post-war Restoration left Scotland impoverished and insecure, and the discovery of oil in the 1970s came too late for the country to yet again reinvent itself. The Oil Wars with Norway and Iceland saw the tenacious Darien Spirit cited for the last time by the nation's first female premier, Margo MacDonald, as the limited naval resources of the nation contested for a share of the new world market.

FROM *War-Songs of the Nation's Favourite, Lena Martell*

One well at a time, Sweet Jesus,
That's all our navy defends,
Just give us the strength to pump all the oil on which we depend,
Shetland is gone, Sweet Jesus,
and Orkney may not hold the line,
Help Margo today
to blow up Norway
one fjord at a time...

A Dichting wi Wahrheit

'ubi solitudinem faciunt, pacem appellant'

Oors wiz the furst bank stood aside –
while roguies hagglet and Scotland cried
       tae coont thi cost o Darien –
Oor ain braw Company bereft,
thi nation noo hud naethin left
       but tae creh utsel 'barbarian'
and bend thi knee tae English sneers
    since naewan else wad back us
wi tares fur beres, wi tears we speired
    is Fletcher oor Calgacus?
         Frae greetan tae weepin
            translatit debt's ochone,
         as Greek yins gae seekin
            oot Deutsche Bankers' loans.

Sae Capital declares utsel
as independent as did Hell
       fae Heiven's stupit rule
that meanin mind thi hert o worth
thi wey thi Pole Star minds thi North
       or ilka ship's a fule.
Calgacus' messages reply
    thru wunds that score auld stanes,
till clishmaclavers thru thi rye
    souch *laive oor land alane.*
         But bankers, lyk anchors,
           keep ilka ship fae sea:
         all bought lands, lyk Scotland,
           maun learn tae pey thir fee.

Dichting: wiping, cleaning; *roguies:* little rogues; *bere:* barley; *speired:* asked;
greetan: weeping; *ochone:* lament; *wunds:* winds; *clishmaclavers:* little whispers,
rumours; *souch:* sigh; *ilka:* each.

Pilgrim Street

2 Οὐδείς

As is our wont I went wrong somewhere, lost
my bearings, drive and hair – and didn't care.
I lived among the anecdotalists,
the giant babies and the well-prepared –
those lappers-up of milk who never share,
those darlings who use talent like a fist.
Out cold so long I thought myself sleep's heir,
I haunted my ambition, some dumb ghost
persisting when its family has left
the building: like an old card stuck to a reused gift.

Part of the art of pilgrimage accounts
viz. Chaucer, Basho and Byron, is the way
that characters or people (these amount
to much the same from far enough away)
actually go to places – as you may
have noticed, in these stanzas journeying's
more meta- than it's geo-: mere display,
these off-Spenserians are travel bling;
Vuittons that voice while other poems look,
recitative within an operatic book.

What is it that these caravans convey
but choral commentary? That 'tell not show'
the orthodox can't bring themselves to say
nor radicals allow themselves to know.
What is the news from no one? Let it go:
your argument's with Yeats, not with the self;
art's brief, it's comprehension that's so slow.
Let others smash your vanity like Delft;
doubt ego into nothingness, confess
to everywhere and no one; neither blast nor bless.

Because the huge dumb effort made to master
everything shoved into my lines of sight,
scent, sound and touch, keeps flailing, I'm a plaster
of jade and jaded – played-out, over-bright.
Meanwhile my family of themes must fight
through jute and ice-floes, jumbling into gray –
plasticene's rainbow, porridge viewed at night –
my thankless crank invention kept from day
by those who play more focussed melodies:
ambition's route one dogmas sound great in journalese.

The contrast is Sibelius and Mahler:
the nation in a synaesthetic note,
then silence; or the symphony's mad sailor
who's fool enough to build a flooded boat
then let his leitmotifs escape its throat
in bubbles, doves and flotsam, unicorns
in bottles, crows – whatever stays afloat
till taste's neap-tide can toss it on its horns.
Time cuckolds both types with posterity
largesse won't second-guess nor will austerity.

The contrast is neat Chopin, lavish Liszt:
the quickie Minute Waltz or *Les Années
de Eurosprawled Pelerinage* – the quest
or the quintessence; 'little corpse' or 'play
it differently again, "threefold" Orphée'.
The contrast is kerygma or the Kirk:
how gnosis only knows what it can't say,
while dogma's only silence is the smirk.
But those who tucked Liszt's butts between their breasts
knew sometimes a cigar is... I forget the rest.

Travel beyond your reputation's pale,
that limited and limiting domain
where few lights blink at your departing sail
as concave as an eyelid. Dark explains

by swallowing your craft from aft to name:
Ulysses' only freedom was to pass
beyond the expectations of his fame
into a sea that shattered guilt like glass.
From '*Οὐδ*' to '*εἰς*' his conscience was released
to splice his vanity to pieces and to peace.

3 METANORTH

Something really does happen to most people who go
into the north…

GLENN GOULD, *The Idea of North*

Domededovo

So this was what it meant to be a child:
time restored to its proper immensity
as though each metre of the airport was
a second, and pacing it from end to end
could make the minutes drag themselves, reluctant,
into dusty hours. I people-watched myself
into misanthropy: long-coated women
clutching each other as they passed on thin legs,
their faces wider, more impassive;
men who would not remove their sealskin caps,
those knotted bear paw pods that perched upon them
even when they ate. Stray beehives passed
in search of swarms, suitcases were so wrapped
in plastic they became oblong cuts of meat.
And everywhere this calm maturity,
that disputatious bulge of eye remembered
from my father's old best friend, as though
the two fingers missing from his machinist's hands
could be at home here, strolling past the check-ins,
crossing a snoozing priest before the icons
in the chapel, nestled in a bath
of moist tobacco I'd not yet discovered
as I paced the gift shops, priced the dolls, and went
outside to risk arrest and photograph
the four prop Aeroflot which poses at the entrance,
to check the chill among the smokers, eye
the peeled-back layers of impacted snow,
and in again, and past the flower stands
and newspapers that restored my grandmother's shop,
its already rotting odour, letters unscrambling
as I learned to read the headlines once again –
Вам придётся ещё немного подождать:
'You just haven't earned it yet baby,'
sitting again and again in the same seat
always beside a different British couple,

'You must suffer and cry for slightly longer'
and watching one of these transient mothers feed
her delighted daughter something mashed and orange,
following her gaze as she craned her neck and chewed
and the great wave of roof unfolded endlessly above her.

Вам придётся ещё немного подождать: You'll have to wait a little longer.

Half a Moon

I awake in the middle of the night air
and out of the window's aspirin
see half a moon, vertically sliced.
I lean and look down on the steppe,
Siberia as husband to that old solitaire –

though here's a hog's hair score of road,
a bunch of lights like spiders' eyes,
and there's a river frozen like a thigh
pressed against some glass as though
it could push through winter into life.

Dawn begins to face down the sectioned moon,
and there are trees that tilt until instead of points
they're sudden shafts, flanking as we dip
onto morning as a landing strip.

Ruchnaya Klat

I have no baggage to reclaim.
Because the driver couldn't know this
he waits at another door, leaving me
aimless in the freezing lovely dawn.

A magpie dips across the icy road
as we skite cautiously for Tomsk.
It's March and everything feels pink as an ear
even the light is peeled as it passes between
the crumbling cylinders of silver birch.

We pass a town called Apryel
as if spring has been stored
and will be released like pigeons or a sickness
when those different needs arise.

The suburbs shift uncertainly between
Mister Pizza's latest concrete hut
and Tomsk's old timber houses
whose filigreed window frames dangle
with shabby icicle thermometers.

At the traffic lights a man crosses
pulling a little roughwood sled
filled with four empty water cooler bottles
as if he's been distilling air.

Just before the hotel we pause opposite
a frozen fair, the carousel horses not quite
clearing their perfect round of snow.

When I get out of the cab only the bag
in my hand stops me floating away.

Ruchnaya klat: hand luggage.

Hotel Bessonnitsa

After a sleepless night, the body weakens.
It grows dear, not one's own, it's nobody's...

Sometimes you're slid beneath the lid
of sleep as though below the ice
that locks the river and you see
it's like a thousand layers of
old paper: wrapping paper like
a mulch of stars, old newsprint in
too many scripts, and letters
in half-recognised, half-strangers' hands
like decades of wallpaper
but without the wall –

and then you're back
and floating in the bed
like a boneless creature in
a depth so dark it cannot see
how white it has become

and memory floats in the body
like an oil that slicks
all surfaces, silencing their birds

and family floats in the memory
like roots in peaty water, everyone
washing away in the speeding flow.

As a coffin floats in the earth
weighed down only by its corpse
so the bed floats in the depths of night
rising slowly with the turning world
towards the surface of the dawn.

To Tomsk! To Tomsk!

The spirit of Elena Shvarts, condemned
to exile from Saint Pandemonium,
considered purgatorial Tashkent –

her angel thought it too Akhmatova;
so, pissing off to Pskov? Way too Pushkin.
They studied Levitan's low road into

Siberia, the convicts' way, discussing Omsk –
very Dostoevsky. So it came to pass,
a year or two before she died, they packed

her soul into my sleeping gear and sent
us on a flight to Tomsk – that little twin
to his House of the Dead; another Athens

because it has six universities,
or university-like things, though none
are near the TranSiberian railway line;

where Chekhov paused en route to Sakhalin
to pour contumely upon its bourgeoisie –
so she, Elena of the fifth of Troys,

could check out if an afterlife spent here
would be completely sleepless in a shtetl,
dull as a dacha, hell on ice. It was.

From the Insomniac's Almanac

1 *The Eyeshades Blink*

We feel like a moustache of midnight cloud
that has somehow slid from a tyrant's lip
and spent months flying here and there
above the forests as they sank into snow,
above the rivers as they froze into swans' necks,
beneath the moon we watched divide like an egg,
like a cyclopic eye becoming two,
and one lens landed here, smothering all growth
beneath this ceaseless blast of plain,
and then we settled on this brow, these eyes.

We are still the ghost of that steel moustache
and have spent decades floating across the steppes
blinding their drunks that plunge into drifts
and emerge in the morning without arms or feet;
or only surface in Spring
when the brushstroke of the river flows again,
faces like the fungus on a log,
the last thing they embraced
the glass root of an empty bottle.

2 *The Earplugs Whisper*

We like to think we glow yellow in the bed-gloom
warning all dins to keep their distance
all ruckus to be remote
He rolls us like a wrap of tobacco
to make us slender as birches
then returns us to our proper shells.
Here is where we ought to live, within
earshot of his never-resting sea.

Timber House, Tomsk

The old house floats upon the frozen earth
like a severed head, its timbers blackened,
dusty with the cold. Icicles like eyebrows tug
down from its eaves and the frames
of its windows are lacy carvings
that soften the determination of the larch.
Its log ends line up neatly like the buttons
on a frock coat on a limbless torso,
but a century of melts and reformation has
unsettled its thoughts until its lintels and its shed
sit at all angles like the exhausted or the shot
making with its neighbours a persistent flotilla
of decapitations huddled in the curve
between the frozen river and the fort.

Lament for Elena Shvarts

I haven't been here for seven hundred years
but nothing has changed.

AKHMATOVA

Elena of the ocean floor of oblast after frozen oblast,
Omsk receding in the troika's rearview mirror,
Tomsk shrugged off like furs from a restless leg of defrosting river,
snowscooters scuttling like white shrimp between
the red cigarette tips of factories like black smokers
in the trenches that scar the abyssal plain.

Your remains remain for me two books in English
and two glances: a shrug across the Baltika and *cherniy hleb* picnic
at Tsarskoye Selo – Pushkin Town, Akhmatova's childish home –
at your refusal to emerge from the shadows on the palace balcony
and read; and my guilty face's reply five years later, shy
at the bar in the Galway Cúirt, that I couldn't talk to you.

Elena, pressed between two covers of urinary ice like amber
and dragged like a Kirghiz princess in search of more
permanent frost – NovoPetersburg, NovonovoMoskva,
NovonovonovoKonstantinople, retreating with the mammoth
toward the Bering Strait, seeking out the Pole's vicegerent,
the Ivory Horn, the frozen Hellespont that Byron skated over.

In the court where Mandelshtam survived, borne against
the current of Vtoraya Rechka, a bubble up Kamchatka's vein,
where Gumilev dodged the bullet, where Irina thrived,
where Shostakovich's seven operas stand in for hills
beneath the purple of the Aurora Imperialis,
Konstantine upon his throne flanked by walruses.

Within the Kremel of Wrangel you shall be wrapped
in the tobacco fur of timber wolves; vodka glasses fashioned from
the thumbs of megatheria sent as tribute from the Inca
shall be placed within your pen-indented fingers –
'hands, matches, an ashtray,' as Akhmatova said;
bears with bloody haloes shall sing your benedictions.

Lyric nun who knew how faithless we are to ourselves,
who discovered the hunger of the full and the fullness of the hungry;
markswoman who sank Peter like a bronze berg, a horseman into
the marsh of the heart, who terrified the Commissar of misprints,
Tutivillis himself; who heard what the rat whispered into
the nautilid's ear – at your funeral even the birds are drunk;

the grasses, like billions of quills, tuck their nibs in
the intolerant steppe and become punctuation: the sough
of commas lamenting their dead words passes here
and there as though the golden herds could learn regret,
as though a woman, pacing in a narrow room,
decided she would never sleep again.

Wrangel Island

14C data thus indicated that mammoths became extinct, even in the refugia of the continental Siberian Arctic, ca. *9.7-10 ka ago. However, in 1990, our first five dates for mammoth remains from Wrangel Island were all of Holocene age, ranging from 7390-4740 BP (Vartanyan* et al. *1992). This surprisingly young estimate prompted us to continue investigations at that location.*

RADIOCARBON, 37, No 1, 1995, pp. 1-6.

I will arrive in darkened, snow-drowned air –
the helicopter larynx, throaty with light,
and everything a silence and a night
compared to when we came from: just the gale
and shuddered, pluming breath, the lurch of waves
that chew on ice and never see a sail.

A bleary lightening means Spring, but still
there's no relief, for all I hear them fill
the slowing evening with their whale-like spray
of kinship calls, and sometimes almost feel
them brush between the walls of our torn tents,
they keep their shrewd millennial distance.

This is the last inch, chosen by extremity,
in which their bones, their ivories, their pelts,
gut contents, piteous calves, shall be preserved:
beyond my lenses' grasp they'll bend their knees.
Meanwhile they shun our fires, our long descent
into the furies that will wipe the earth clean.

Pilgrim Street

3 *Icarious*

How many lives divide in three like mine?
Winging it, my trajectory got broken
Apollo–Houston-problem style, the line
went down for years of drift, till I'm rewoken
from stasis for a new career as token
creative in a school of brittle stiffs.
But for the first part, how it seemed unspoken:
literature, love, and love of Italy, gifts
that meant the Grand Tour should have been resumed
upon re-entry to a small Venetian room.

Mosquitos whined like my old nightly rages,
the canaletto echoed my retreat:
I'd be the father, figuring his wages,
who holidays in post-ambitious Crete,
Chania, where on a still-Venetian street,
coiling between an icon – Agios Giorgios –
and Casa di Pietro's stairwell peek
at Artemis in marble – fake, but gorgeous –
like Actaeon on ouzo, I ask the saint
how long you last with dragons gnawing at your paint?

While in that middle stretch, those seven years
of beautiful myopia that filled
with monsters far less frightening than peers,
it felt like we, gone wrong, were being filmed:
as partners parted, beds skewed, psyches spilled,
this was a movie no one else could see –
the same one Tzanes caught in oil, his still
in which God's hand commands the kill, and we
observe St George's armoured arm obey;
the snake head pinned, the globe-arsed horse half-turned away.

Old paintings like to bother me: one crude
scene nags, as though pile-driven down dream-deep:
white penitents process in pointy hoods
across the dark canals as though asleep;
crocodile through back *calles*, try to keep
out of the city's knowing drench of light.
I used to line up empties like glass sheep,
and mock my dog-like thirst – old appetite –
by popping done crisp packets on their heads –
numb echo of that dumbed repentance of the dead.

That dunce-self I'd escaped, or so I thought,
into the hides of books, still starcs back through
the pages of their print-smeared *capirote*,
it gets by on my pride in what I do –
that sound between the truth and sounding true
which Guston's stubbly Klansmen (Nixons, hoods,
lynch parties lunked in lethargy) all knew:
most artists would look pretty in good in snoods –
the mirror in their heads, not on the wall,
tells them it's better to be nobody at all.

I tried to be the Sci-Fi afterlife
of presbyters, the whisper of a Pict;
the baddest of mock poets north of Fife,
a shaman (also bad), a Dardan sect;
one of the cybernetically Elect,
a surgeon (mad), a Lakeside idiot,
several horses; first Herebericht,
then Wedderburn – two priests within one Prod.
Somewhere between my ego and this verse,
Nobody has usurped my tiny universe.

Nobody is the lens through which we glimpse
the Cyclops' eyeball skewered on a caber –
that whale harpooned by five translucent shrimps,
great Duellist nicked by gnat-cloud, clutching sabre.

Nobody is the giant's ideal neighbour –
silver banana medallist, mere sub:
a great man only names his greater faber
when laurel-strewn or eyeless in the pub.
Do you aspire to rank nonentity?
Then join our club: a crew that never goes to sea.

4 MANY BLACK COUNTY

To make the poem work in English I had to change
everything: the plot, characters and outcome, in order
to give a sense of the original.

GWYNETH LEWIS

Night Drive to Many-black County (黟縣)

Rushing in the six hour night drive
from Shanghai to Huangshan
beneath billboards for *Crystal Fowl*
warnings of *Rain and Fogy Weather*
the minibus fills with a chilled two note drone
as in the 70s TV show where this announced
the apparition of a UFO
a ritual of warm-canned *Tsingtao*
and stopping for a piss on perspex
beneath which some actual lilies do not toil
the hills an edgeless hunch except
when lit from behind by puppet spacecraft landing
when they become a jetsam of mashed pagoda
an orange sickle moon above the 'restrooms'
holds back the jet-lag as if a hand could hold
a whole forest severed at its base

I buy a plastic goldfish on small wheels
that bolts when you pull its string
the bamboo dream grows fast
pine-fresh metaphysic I watch a hand
writing to the glow of a mobile phone
in worm calligraphy 'the darkness is not
a nothingness   its silence holds each sound
by the suicidal wrist
it grips the unanswered prayer
consider what happens when you split
the character 竹 (*zhú*)
from bam to boo'
I don't know what happens
and no one I ask knows either
'nothing is not an empty something
eternity is not a very long time'

I'm looking through contact lenses
made of mother of pearl at
some up-jutting antenna, its base half-visible
so the bullshead frame hangs thirty feet up
late bicycles, former bicycles, suicidal bicycles
the hole in the beer-can like a bicycle saddle
occasional unshuttered shops
the uncombed man sitting on the pavement outside a garage
the reedy river a light moves down
more like a waterfowl than a reflection
walls of houses reflected on unrippling dead water
so that the crash barrier casts a level shadow
that seems to cut their chalky bellies in two
roofs begin to bow in the middle
like saddles seen in profile, fields are manes and tails
entrances gored with sag-horn water buffalo porticoes

having arrived in the Ming Dynasty
breathing a green liquid
we forget what a bus is for and continue on foot
black of the mountain
black of the inkstone
my father is weak and cannot continue
black many 　　黟 (Yi)　　the fire radical
to the left of the gate the characters say
the sea wind cannot find the river
to the right
the both hands cannot find the arse
night is a brushstroke the size of the paper
the darkness multiple 　　黟
perfectly at home inside each head it carries
it carries on
we carry on carrying it through the dark

74

Translating the Yellow Mountain

1

An audacity of naming drove the Daoists up
Huangshan; flocking like the luck of magpies
they escaped there with our silver spoon of speech,
feet barely scraping the spatulate, stilt-walk peaks.

Adamic mynahs, shamanic climbers,
they've left us clasping at the wake of nomenclature,
leaning on entwined pine-trunks
they claimed were long-spined lovers,

looking down at dragon claws
they saw instead of roots, wordless
at dusk's arrival, submerged in the heights' fog
we mob the entitled rocks, dry as crows.

2

They turned the corners of paths down
like pages on two thousand year drops
and made the mountain script,
the cloud a calligraphy, which,

because the camera is smaller than the eye,
we cannot read. Pinnacles were pens, resting in
the gaps between us, pocketed
on empty breasts, left in absent desks.

A tree sprouted from one nib
like ink into an ocean. Declared a poem,
it dispersed and was translated into a plastic replica
redrafted as yet another tree.

3

Too cold at sunset and too warm at dawn
I miss their herded stars, that squatting ape-rock

staring at its favourite metaphor, the mist-flood
which brims horizons with a breathable sea,

and settle for crowds, jammed at noon,
as sun-visored potentates are
borne past on springy bamboo litters
on steps that drape the slopes like bandoliers

by porters who must bear
all garbage and all goodness
shuddering up and dumbly down
our dynasties of later.

4

A flight of four clouds circles
the mountaintop, feathers burning off
in the noonday sun as we discuss
their suitable subjects for poetry,

a not-disallowed roofbeam
of further cloud supports the east.
Their stylitic immortals ignore us,
play chess in slow eroded gambits

while our brethren nap with baseball caps
pushed back, sprawled by a narrow path
hooked through the so-called jaw
of a colossal river fish.

5

Korean ahoys cross the voids,
police squat on overhangs, directing traffic;
we shriek in queues on steep paths
like martins on a wire, ignore in turn

the clear signal of coins in a green pond
glinting and wishing by the wayside,
the slivered sheet of light between
a leaning ton of stone and its elder, the cliff.

We cross the footbridge hung with lovers' padlocks.
For some reason we refuse
to fling our books into the depths.
For some reason we refuse to fling ourselves.

6

Dawn-risen dough of stone, baked cinnamon
by afternoon, butts our brows against
the lowering sun, so I come down from the mountain
a prawny hothead, monkey-browed,

their anthology of lotus lithos and turtle beak
published upon my skull as though a stele
fell there from that stellar raft
they stepped on onto when

they decided they should name
the hind-quarters of the heavens,
when they questioned whether the stars
were even facing us.

7

As if a ghost of their name-calling still directs
the fondness of the eye we see
as we descend an obelisk as mobile phone
monocerous with aerial.

Beside this, as we squeeze
into the final tunnel – or, for those who climb
to meet us here, the first – a butterfly
flies at or into my ear.

It sounds white, but with the mountain
outlined across its wings,
and in this momentary darkness I inherit
its uric stink of printing and am home.

Facts about Pigs

Pigs believe they are in a forest
at all times, it's just that the trees
have gotten very far apart.
Pigs really do eat shit
it's just that they prefer prosciutto.
They believe in acorns
and that trees poop truffles.

According to pigs
humans are vertical swine,
dolphins are merely seaswine.
Pigs are not for roses
rings are not for noses
pokes
are for folks.

If my father tickles a pig
along the coarse hairs of its spine
it falls into a trance
and can be made to believe
its trotters are stuck together hands
can be made to believe
it is a real man.

Here is a pig lullaby
I once heard a sow
sing to a row of piglets
as she ate them:

Ruskin's buskins
Tuskalorum
Mishkin's Pushkin
Luskentyre.

Rustum's lustrum
in the forum
Munchkin's lunchkin –
Mummy's tired.

The hog I saw
on the back of a motorbike
in Guangzhou,
traveling astonished
in a cylindrical frame

laterally, so that, as we overtook
I could look
into its still-living face,
believed it could fly
but seriously did not want to.

The Tomb

To make a mountain out of a manhole,
the earth slit that commands us enter
and be still
        then lose it
for two thousand years
in the centre of the city of Guangzhou.

To embed within this mound,
written in the fetid ink of air
    with corridors for downstrokes
    chambers for their blotting ends,
the character for 'warrior'
                        土 (*shi*)
    when you couldn't finish
your grandad's fifty year old fights.

For these burrows to stand and fall
    for shrine and throne room, kitchen, store,
compressing palace into warren
as the Nanyue Dynasty was wedged
    into the shoe of five generations
tripping over your fratricidal grandkids.

To require two guards to kneel behind the door
    sealed with a fungal glyph, sunk into the rock;
that chamberlain left in the hall
    to guide any visiting immortals
into the room of rotting concubines
away from the quarters where a cook
    and two musicians sprawl
among the hambones, flutes and ladles.

For them all to be buried alive
because you were too grand to go alone
into the big dark hill
                        in your little jade suit
of ten thousand pills.

I do not like you, green lobsterman,
        though not even your dust remains,
just the blades and copper livery,
                        goblets and bells
that tell of open moments, mouths and eyes
you passed on for your mercury tonic,
        nightcap that ushers
        all the desperate emperors
        into their huddled forevers.

Atlantic College

1

I open my curtain and the horse walks by
moving through the trees as though
it were a tree, a shadow in their shade.

Is it Severn and Somerset gleaming as though
a vertical strap between the trunks, a belt
buckled with abalone, a girdle of watered sun?

I have mountains to ink in before I can swim.
The ocean depths that link us won't fathom
themselves; the block requires uncarving.

Much later on the crows announce
the procession of a single goat, thicket-crowned
and queenless, entering his columned court.

2

As I pad on tiptoe through the early rain
the heels of my new deckshoes rust with blood,
tear off the scabs from the backs of my old ankles
as though I lost my shadow there
from those two tendons' seams.

3

A newly-discovered path to the swimming pool
divides the pregnant stars on the flanks of the cows

from the already tick-gathering lambs,
the just-delivered ewes.

Mist from Porlock fills the Channel
and eats the cows, their field, this fence.

4

Before we can see Sir John's Hill, Wang Xaoni
is translating a poem of mine – its roadside Horus
into the assassin who chased the First Emperor
around his pillared throne-room, from which
his watching guards were barred all entry
while the Great Unifier tried, all out of breath,
to draw too long a sword from its sheath.

5

And what does the mist call but when
are you coming down
off Yellow Mountain and back
to Atlantic College in the rain

stanzas like gondolas

What does the rain advise
but rush from that castle
its siege by school dinner
and make for the back-road

axis tilted into telpherage

And where could this road
hind-leg of a stallion
lead you, far from umbrellas,
but to this hoof of a bar

descent through diagonal dragon rocks

Where could it strike you
but square on the forehead
Porlock's the emperor
that we interrupt

the lion-headed hills aslant

6

'The eagle/hawk in [her now-hybridised here-there] sky
flies/shears across the hedge [resisting my
line-ending] to suddenly stop [still] held there by
an urgent need on that scissor-edge: the silhouette
of Jing Ke taking to the road, the [archaic] character
for 'Kill' carved into the bamboo edict
that deathly wish [an emphasis that works well in Chinese].
There is a lock, the hawk/eagle is continually
like a key, it must release that narrow death
from everywhere in air [her allusion sexualising the line]
He is a tender dagger that must stab.'

7

Raiser of the wall, burner of all books,
placer of cosmos inside tomb inside China inside cosmos,
Kaiser of all characters ranked in ink: beware.

Beside you   who is there
in the sea mist that counts you in
mountain fog that counts you out

8

Everything ends badly for everyone except the hawk
still blazing in the low Laugharne air:
the slow vole at the foot of his regard
is Yang Lian's car being lifted by the slope-eating tide.

And the film company, trying to film
the locals of Laugharne attempting to recite
'Do not go', told us – a gaggle of bards, flam's flims,
word-peregrines – to be quiet.

Meanwhile the cantor of our apocalyptic hawk,
translator of brown ale, horse of the closed hotel,
perched on drainpipe heron legs in his study,
moves his mind's nib upon the uncrumpling page.

Time, translated into assassin yet again, tracks
like a shadow, backs away from duty. Death is on pause.

9

The grave a Gothic font upon a trim white cross
pressed into a breast of hillside striped in darker stones
so no one could fail to find them both and leave him there

a miniature white horse, hoof raised as though it only had
three shoes, a miniature of Red Label, faded,
a jar of begonias, white heather – all the Scotch

allusions crashing like bottles into recycling drums
in the carpark below. The chaffinches are filling the yews
with their truncation of song the way this grave is filled

with their marriage. I unpocket that unlikely fig
I picked up like a blackened dewdrop by
the castle wall, and give it, rest it with the rest.

10

And so the Person came
on its great bamboo stilt legs
across the Channel, across the Atlantic,
and stabbed him through the brain.

'There's learning for you, there's knowledge
neither pain nor gain stops me
where I come from precedes all chickens
and sucks the teaching from all eggs.'

The Attributes and Martydom of St Donat

Patron saint of St Donat's or Llandunwyd, Glamorgan, Wales.
Nothing else is known, but in some lists he is called Dunwyd.

1 *What are the attributes of St Donat?*

No one knows the legend or the gender of St Donat
not even St Donat. Once while he was heading
to the pub down the deerhound's leg of the lane
around by Atlantic College, haired with long rain
and brushed by late hares, he saw ahead
of his head a fried dough halo, a *churro* torus
softer than the sort the Greeks call koulouri,
cloudier than what the Ashkenazi term *pretzel*,
which the Americans call
Halitosis the President-Choker.

It was an ecumenical pub, selling the ales
of Wales and Cornwall; his pals were all there
with their long lances like pens upon which they had speared
little scops owls, boopers of the night fields,
drinking the beers from Aberystwyth to Zennor.

Especially pissed owls were placed like tiny hassocks
for the silver knees of devout but adventurous children
along a high shelf. He thought
perhaps his vision had only been an owl
with a hole in its heart, perhaps
from flying between the flank of Christ
and the javelin of a kindly legionnaire,
that the sugar sprinkles on its upper slopes
might indeed have been the tears of our Lord.

He wondered whether, when St Thomas had placed
his hand in Christ's bloodied side,
he had pulled out an owl?

2 *Yes, but what are his or her attributes?*

His attributes are the small doughnut van
left at an angle in unsuccessful fairs
or prayer meetings, in deserted late night streets
or, closed, in the carparks of unmanned railway stations.

Inside, the miracle of halos
dropping into fat continues to sizzle
as though clouds, turned gold by evening,
felt God's finger poke through their innards
and fell immediately into the Atlantic,
bobbing there for years like giant lifebelts
with guano for icing, and studded with fallen flares.

Pilgrims may avail themselves of any pierced disk
as a token of their journeying, such as small floats
snipped off fishermen's nets, or printed targets
worn with holes shot approximately through their hearts,
or mints, the rings of Saturn (minus Saturn,
naturally), cyclones seen from above,
maelstroms seen from below, or,
ideally, a doughnut.

Often, when done with all that, St Donat would sit
with his arm round a lighthouse, looking out
to the West, and wonder what gender
he actually was, and how
his martyrdom would finally come:
by deep fat fryer like that episode of *Spooks*?

Or would he be smothered in tyrannical icing
like a blanket of sweet snow, a pillowcase
filled with the feathers of a million owls?

Zennor Wat

Zennor is a sleepy question: by the tiny chapel what
did Lawrence dream its timber mermaid was asked
in fisherman and tinner's hymn? The coast's all cost,
its skies all whys, its bays are question marks in sand,
interrogants in granite. Befitting a curious fish,
Gurnard's Head shovels its hill-fort pout into the ocean.

There Graham wintered in abstraction's caravan –
poor as a petrel peering through the fo'c'sle's pane,
proud as wren-song where the foxglove nods –
just down from the dolmen, not far from the mine-shaft
Lowry sketched in '57, though they never met, its pit
the left boot of Carn Galver, the right lost in the ocean.

I cross the trench where the slingsmen stepped to shoot
and clamber upon spreadeagled outcrops, then out
onto the lowering brow of the fish: sea pressed
upon by light, the canopy of February
tucked three miles out beneath a mattress
of unanswerable, sleepless and bedazzled ocean.

Dead Mole

(after a photo by Pamela Robertson-Pearce)

Sprawling in an indent on a drystane dyke,
cast there by the moleman, mowdie-murderer,
as though it were a turf, the mitt a walker lost:
the mole, stone-dead but like it's crawling still
through air, claws freckled with dirt, its soot frame
a stockinged foot pulled from the long shoe of earth,
its chest a wee barrel of muscle, a loutish no-neck,
mouth a perfect A of teeth and whiskery chin,
snout made blunt by thrusting into dark
and the inert turned homely, wormless, dry;
it lies as though sodden with the fact of soil,
deafened by the bass note of the grave, drowned
by blueness, thrown spaldered and absurd
as if downed drunk with singing of our end.

Eschatology of the Fly

Why did you do me downward as I dithered by,
dozy as a dachshund in the warm mid-air?
On the fifth lap of the kitchen, then, you caught me out,
smacked me with the whammy of your flat moon-mace.
You broke my gallant topsail of the sheeniest glass,
shattered every pane upon my mizzen mast,
as well as stoving in my stubbled fur-box ribs,
so that I lay along the painted concrete floor
and panted as I pedalled at the lower nocht
as though it were a bike, and saw the ceiling be
the bottom of the clearest deepest sea all set
for my abrupt departure. Was it exercise
or envy or the chance to try your giant eye
and flex your long slow arm against my circuitry?

Come with me now into the after-tunnels where
gravestones stick like eggs against the worm-built walls
and larva struggle in their sticky shrouds for air.

In winglessness we must crawl in these gutters up
through the seepage of the silage and your honey tears,
sometimes across the tin gut's floor and sometimes on
the grey intestine's roof tiles where we'll tattoo out
dead mariachis in our tap shoes till at last we meet
a porter of those stoppered parts, who sizes you
for seizing or for ease of the innoculant –
and so appears behind you with the needle's push
into your lolly headpiece like a long sharp hair,
then the nulling of your dream of only being you
begins just like a bleaching of your nasal stems:
wasabi-eucalyptus then the lung-green pin
porcupines the passages behind your eyes
till what you are can't get away from all you're not.

And then you're just some runnel-scurf and well-chewed wax
they roll in grit and grease until you globulate
as jubejubes for their ratty daughters that depend
among the ribcage webs – one eyelash all you've left
and all it knows of ways to go is up the shaft,
the bones all scratched with charms in every lingo known,
with canting old confessions, incorrect accounts,
commandments in such characters as brook no doubts
though nobody can read them now their lights are out.

And everywhere the twining worm and rusty ant
and everywhere the bat's crapped and the white owl flits
until the collarbones patrolled by dragonflies
where mantises catch hold of you like prayerwheels
and pop you in that hive-head of the rolling eyes –
Beelzebub the brilliantined colossal lord
surveys this middle realm through every aperture
that's opened to him through your artful wantonry
and watches you as closely as the One above.

Did you suppose we didn't have necropoli –
a species focussed so upon the nethers' flux?
That nobody could judge you as you broke the bread
I'd crawled across and emptied out my juices on?
A million small communions each compose our world,
and mean we all share constantly the joyous feast
and once we are consumed we share a common dream.

Blootered Bloomsbury Blues

I used to look like Dylan
but now I look like dull,
some people make a killing
while others make a skull.
My left rib's started floating
and it gives my gut the hex
it feels as though it's voting
to be some other sex.
These are the just-scootered-in
semi-blootered Bloomsbury blues

I was walking in a circle
all around St George's Church
a gopura's on that kirk all
the gods left in the lurch.
I went into a reading,
heard a poet shake her reed:
but when all the bats are feeding
it's a bad idea to bleed.
These are the rough, untutored
blootered Bloomsbury blues

The Brits have a Museum
because they lack a Muse
but it doesn't do to tease them
about things that just confuse.
Their scholars keep on scraping
while the spirits all escape
and the icons they are raping
have their honey-traps on tape.
This is the second shooter of
the blootered demi-Bloomsbury blues

I met Philip Nikolayev
and we drank with Yang Lian –
you can splash mud in your eye if
you don't want to understand,
but from Cambridge to Calcutta
and New Zealand to Hong Kong
we could hear the people mutter
'We do not need your song.'
This is the unsuitable suitor of
the blootered Bloomsbury blues

Let the poet leave his body
like whalemeat to the Queen;
leave anthologies to Roddy –
it's just rude to intervene.
From London to Siberia
from Tomsk unto Beijing
if they think your air superior
the people will not sing.
This is the randomising router of
the hemi-blootered Bloomsbury blues

Since you cannot find *agape*
you can only mind the gap
between the happy-clappy
and the oligarchs of rap.
It's when nobody is seeing
all the things you think you know
that you hit them with the feeling
that you plainly cannot show.
this is the computer virus called
blootered Bloomsbury Blue

But now I'm on a stipend
when I used to be like Stipe:
some talents can be ripened
while some others taste like tripe.
Each boy sets out by roaring
he's a little emperor;
each man ends up ignoring
he's become a little whore.
this is the well-armed looter entitled
blootered Lemmy-hits-Bloomsbury Blue

Tiresias is Tracey
or at least he has her tits,
Catullus had a crazy
dream of cutting off his bits.
Whether willing or unwilling
you must do the poem's will:
I used to look like Dylan
but now I must kill Bill.
These are the crudely-neutered
blootered Bloomsbury blues

The Chinataur

soon after this debacle found himself
  in tunnels lined with crockery, shelf
after shelf of chipped and half-remembered sets
  of saucers, fruit bowls, dinner plates:

a coffee cup that, once in childhood, held
  to the now-occluded sun, revealed
a brittle geisha haloed by its base –
  where had he drunk in that drowned face?

a soup bowl landscaped with grey cherry trees,
  the bridge that wished to be Chinese
from which all cuckolds, lovers, cooing birds
  were washed away like once-loved words;

the wineglass asterisked in gold as though
  at dawn the stars refused to go;
the sea-deep jug on which some rip-tide hand
  sketched crayfish, but left the shore unpenned.

He wandered for the only hours between
  ghost rows that should be smithereens,
groaned as his skeleton by sharp degrees
  transmuted into cutlery;

smiled at the cellars' sentimental clack,
  his salt-and-peppered scrotal sac,
and wept as one obliged to be reborn
  to feel his new-grown porcelain horns.

Facts about Things

Things are tired.
Things like to lie down.
Things are happiest when,
for no reason, they collapse.

That French plastic bottle, still half-full,
that soft-back book, just leaning on
another book, drowsily:
soon they will want to go outside,

soon you will find them in the grass
with the empty bleaching cans and that part
of an estate agent's sign
that's covered in a fine grime like mascara.

That plastic bag you've folded up
feels constrained by you and wants
to hang from bushes, looking like
a spirit, sprawled and thumbing a lift.

Things are bums, tramps, transitories:
they prefer it when it's raining.
Lightbulbs like to lie in that same
long uncut casual grass

and watch the funnel effect: the way
on looking up the rain all seems
to bend towards you,
the way the rain seems to like you.

Things which do not decay
like it best in shrubbery, they like
to be partly buried.
They like the coolness of the grass.

Most of all, they like it
when it rains.

The Dog

(for Keith Morris)

The dog came down the sidestreet at a trot,
large, utterly silent, headed straight at me
as though it held a herald in its mouth
it would deposit, sodden with saliva, at
my feet. It was way after chucking out,
and we'd been riffing on libretti and
the death of comic opera, though some
of us were busy trying to forget
those things we'd left unsung two decades back
when we were so-called lovely, vague and young.

I knew immediately that it came
from you, despite it having been curled up
inside the Cross Keys earlier that night,
a lanky anchor at its master's heels.
I knew you loved intrusion in your work,
just like at Washingwell, where in the wood
they had commissioned you to celebrate
a sculptor's W in blue, a bridge:
so you hid trumpeters like giant wrens
among the trees, a nest of sudden brass.

The dog looked like it had been pushing through
the reeds we'd watched them burning at
the Maltings, its lank grey coat curling like
the fishhook of its tail. It looked as though
it had been travelling in darkness for
as long as we had known each other, with
the silence of your death held gently in
its mouth as though it were a water bird
it left there in the middle of our lives
for me to find the human echo to.

Dispersing in the grey dog's midnight wake
like unfed gulls among the car-less streets
of silenced Aldeburgh; abandoning
our tricky past like an unfinished meal
as though all crewmanship, all mooring was
unfastened by this passing, we found sleep,
though my way took me past the frozen pond
for toy ships only, and along the height
of shingle that the ceaseless scoring waves
kept drafting in the darkness down below.

Whale Road

Imagine a whale in the street, bruising and blubbering
painstakingly toward the firth, half-flattening the cars
that have been abandoned in its way, their drivers fled
a few yards and then, like you, returning to gove.

It's a street in Edinburgh: you can choose your own –
perhaps in Gorgie, elbow-lessly shoving aside tenements,
or too far down the Lothian Road for hope of cold salt water –
but no, it's the road leading out to the Forth Bridge,

the one that in your vague memory map passes the Zoo,
that bar you think of as Cameron Brig though you know it isn't,
as though all the nasty grain whisky came from one pub.
The whale is tearing itself apart as it heaves painfully ho,

stuck with glass and metal from all the cars, doors open
like insect wings, studded with motorbikes, which, when crushed,
look even more like bluebottles. It looks like an obese kidnap victim,
tied to a small metal chair at wrist and ankle, self-capsized

and trying to drag-crawl himself toward the nearest door.
Of course the door is locked: it's that kind of movie.
It should be stop-start animation, but apart from the pathetic
jerkiness of its locomotion, the whale is all too real,

pushing aside the lampposts like reeds or those palms
that conveniently flatten out sideways when the Traceys launch
Thunderbird Two. Of course that could never get off the ground,
and so too this can't really be happening – perhaps

the proximity of the zoo made you dream it up, the memory
of that elephant seal sat on its elephant seal-sized island
in a *jus* of smelly shat-in water, and the basin wall all round
over which you poked your curious cruel nose.

Couldn't you just have hallucinated a seal in a corridor,
that celebrated one an unidentified uncle brought back
from the whaling and kept in a bath-tub? Couldn't it just have been
a walrus squeezing down that wynd by the Half-Way House,

rather than this massive loose white weight ripping itself open
with every motion, as though a python had swallowed a goat
and now must burst open in a chimeric parody of birth?
You know it will choke under the weight of its organs,

unsupported by the callous air it keeps wheezing in
and drily ejecting through its blowhole – even that
is stentorian, a gross rupturing bagpipe fart
that makes the onlookers recoil a few steps each time,

before coming closer again, like gulls. You know it will expire
under its own weight long before it bleeds to death,
but you still imagine the long road of dark blood behind it.
Soutar's playful whale swims into your head, disgorging

Jonah-like lions and unicorns; you think of McGonagall,
ranting his poem in the yard as they butchered its subject.
But these are just attempts to distract yourself from
what unfolds and refolds in front of you, like a Bible

trying to shuffle itself open at a passage you cannot recall.
What should you do? Call on Ishmael? Isn't he already here?

Pilgrim Street

4 *Katabasics*

Off-centre in the centre of my life –
that's how it's always been: the ideals slip
away, the mastery will not arrive;
while habits fix, reforms refuse to grip.
A daoist vegetarian, too hip
to compromise the future with his vote;
a dope who, vindicated by the trip,
still couldn't tell the ocean from the boat,
got off his floating world, grew backwards to
the family as art, then failed to follow through.

Inventing the vocation in the Haugh,
that cross-roads where a B-road crossed the Urr,
rewired my brain into an anxious loch,
a broth of hypochondria, a blur
through which an ageing doctor wasn't sure
but thought she saw a tumour like a trout.
A night in hospital is not a cure
nor are two tests, then three more months of doubt
before the scan, but as the auld man laughed
at midnight in the worried ward, 'They'll wheech us aff

and cover us in concrete.' Nurses drew
a conference of curtains round his bed
and left us dreamless, lucid, hopeless, new,
in transit through the outlands of the dead.
Mature art meant the carapace was shed –
no aping others' genius, claiming *nous*
while acting like a faithless infant ned:
there was a child that stanzas wouldn't house
but I could hope to father; a career –
the teacher first learns how to leave the House of Fear.

Those nurses and our muses are the same:
they've dealt with us and with the likes of us
before, grand vanities and little shame –
sometimes vice versa, but, whatever, thus
it is with these vile bellies: just adjust
perspective on Parnassus, say the Nine,
and watch us go – first flesh, then rot, then dust;
they overlook the final twitch of lines,
footless as snakes who treat their tails as teats.
Go mouthy or go mute – you go, they wash your sheet.

When I was on the Low Road's darkest patch,
a baby girl upon my shoulders, the cats' eyes
that should have lit its single track all scratched
out by anxiety, I recognised
them as my ancestors', their colour prised
from black and white, my gran's old greeny blue
made cataracted marbles, and surmised
I must still be in hospital, not through
its lidless night, not yet, not waking up
for months, just learning where you go without a map.

When I was on the Silk Road's lowest stretch
between the two oases' green-tiled tombs,
Peach Blossom Paradise beyond our reach
behind the Kunlun's range of grim jade gums
all fanged with ice, our livers had no homes,
our hangovers were nomads and our lights
revolved within our bellies, since our bones
were swopped for sharp dust-devils – in that night
I saw the frightening place I'd visited
back in the Haugh, though like the country of the dead,

was never there at all, instead it was
a Helicon, that habitation next
to clarity, awake to lack of cause
and simple as cold water's lens, its flex
of sunlight in cupped palms. Placed outside text,

103

you watch that scorpion beside your foot
and see it has no goals, is unperplexed
and ready as a sickness. There's no route
that leads to anywhere but here; no shame,
no game: the Silk Road and the Low Road are the same.

5 HOTEL LABYRINTHOS

So now you know…that in Greece when you hear a story, you must expect to hear its shadow, the simultaneous counterstory. Because…we have eaten the six pomegranate seeds here, and all our stories come in two versions, and the story that is told in hell will sound different from the same story as they tell it in heaven.

PATRICIA STORACE, *Dinner with Persephone*

Bull-Leaper

(figurine from the palace at Knossos, 1600–1500 BC)

The Labyrinth is, after all, a room,
left open while, for seven years, the state
must renovate its take on ancient Crete –
we take a half hour per millennium

with frescoed youths, wasp-waisted; pendant bees
in wing-thin gold; small goddesses, breasts bared,
who shake snakes into sigmas – all crammed here
with squid and hippalektryon, all lees

of burnt-out storerooms cornered under vines
grasshoppers slowly climb, to split their skins
and sway, green listeners, their empty twins
dropping, dry to the legs' decanted tines,

the way this metonym for Minos leaps
a now-abstracted bull: small diplomat
in age-striated ivory, it keeps
falling, beyond us, face blank as a cat.

NOTE: Heraklion Archaeological Museum closed for renovation in 2004.
One room is kept open for display. At the time of printing the museum
has not yet reopened.

Dead Villages

Because the needle sharpness of the dark,
its million brilliant pores, means that instead
of puffy orange you can see the trail,
that sky-long cloud of the galactic spill;

because that renovated sky is pitched
above your memories of childish night;
you start to think you're travelling in time
back through rooms pinned to their icons,

towards a coolness somewhere in these hills,
the height of which is only measured by
the constellated legions they eclipse,
those lightless villages you could drive through

knowing your lights would then refuse to find
their silent inhabitants although they sit
outside the empty-glassed cafeneion
or stand below the thirsty walnut trees.

Or so you think as you fold up the sheets
you hung out in the midday heat and then
forgot: they could be gathered here tonight
beneath these still undancing points and looking up.

The Sickle

The second day my hand still trembled from
the sickle. We see it now as attribute,
those ageing symbols' symbol, death and work,
and like to overlook the thing itself,
bulb-handled in warm wood, the cursive blade
a darkened, runnelled metal, cheaply made
and left inside the old tin bath with saws,
fence staples, in the dust-black, padlocked shed
among the furniture and frames thrown out
of the old peoples' version of a home,
the cobwebbed halter for their long-dead mule.
We want to make it moon and question mark,
cedilla of skeletal script, a lip,
but it is quite at ease with all this mess,
the afterlife of things and half-life of
their meanings: it's accustomed to the edge
between the real and the irrelevant.
A little oil would help it sing out as
it's lifted from its bed; serrations, rust,
acknowledge its return to use, to light.
And all I did was cut the long dry grass
behind the outhouse where the washing line
plays out its yellow plastic smile. I took
their three foot nodding lengths in hand,
half baby fishing rods and half the shades
of ostrich feathers, and I hacked them once
or twice, and cut their shins and thistles' throats
until our towels could hang in peace.
And all the time the sickle silently
displayed its neatness, crooking in the strays
and never needing more than three light chops
at any head, and though I cut away
from my leg every time it whispered past
'flesh of my edge, bone of my blade,' and cut
until it was too easy to cut close,
and then I paused, and put the thing away.

The Palikari Scale of Cretan Driving Scales

(all measurements given in large black moustaches)

χωρίς μουστάκι

experiences mild rocket/donkey confusion re αυτοκίνητο (car):
is it a rocket and therefore capable of interstellar travel? OR
is it a donkey and can therefore be stopped in middle of
       thoroughfare
for chats with fellow donkey-owners? δεν ξέρω (I dunno)

μια μουστάκι

regards speed limits, lane markings & traffic lights as thoughtful
       advice;
overtakes all touristicals & farm vehicles immediately without
       regard for oncoming traffic;
wears shades while driving one-handed at night (liberated arm
       must dangle from open window);
experiences rocket/donkey paradox as zen koan rather than safety
       issue

δύο μουστάκια

understands double white line down centre of road = overtake
       faster stripes;
always overtakes on blind corners/summits (wind-surfing arm
       must undulate, snake-like, from window);
observes zero-to one-handed driving plus smoking pre-requisite
       while shouting on mobile phone;
adds shades-wearing angel of death to rocket/donkey conundrum.

τρία μουστάκια

only drives a black, tinted-windowed SUV with speedboat attached;
overtakes when, if at all possible, another SUV is heading towards
car, preferably also overtaking;
is heavily armed/transporting yoghurt/sheep/all of previous (armed
arm must dangle from window, open or not);
finally understands angels, rockets and donkeys have become one
hypostasis.

τέσσερα μουστάκια

travels at speeds far in excess of mere sound so shall never be
heard approaching;
manifests only around the corners of lazy single-track lanes no one
has been seen down for years;
ensures vehicle is four apocalyptic donkey-powered (and glass-
bangled arm has scythe);
has clearly mistaken self for vengeful spirit manifested in aftokinetic
form and winged in moustaches;

πέντε μουστάκια

a driver from Sfakia.

Night Rain in Emprosneros

For once the mountains that peer down through the vine at us
like giant scientists, sheer aunts with pine-pocked octopus skin,
vanished before nightfall behind a mat of tufting grey cloud
we reassured ourselves could not mean rain.

But rain it did, in darkness, hesitantly, as if unsure of protocol,
and scattershot, so that you could hold your hand out
and not feel a drop, while beside you the little flame of the oil lamp
was precisely sizzled out. And start and stoppingly, so that

you couldn't tell whether the towels needed taking in or not
and went and stood beneath the separated-out rain, gauging it.
Then furiously, for five minutes or so, or so the vine leaves claimed,
though that could just have been their patter. Glancing up

between the unripe grapes you saw the white belly of the rat
who visits here by dusk, then moved the white plastic chairs
beneath the plaster eaves, and draped them with the towels,
and filled your lungs with the scent of the astonished earth,

that freshness compacted of dirt and leaf and air, delicious
as chilled fruit, then watched the jasmine flowers being struck
over and over, as though the stars were being stung, then lay down
and listened to the passage of the clouds throughout the night.

Karnagio

A wayfarer will meet you and will say it must be a winnowing shovel
that you have got upon your shoulder; on this you must fix the oar
in the ground and sacrifice a ram, a bull, and a boar to Poseidon.

THE ODYSSEY, XI

Not the *estiatório* beneath the city walls of Chania,
old Kydonia, home of the Cretan quince,
Captain Adam's apple, Diktynna's gift, she
meh eftrafeís gloutoús (with stout buttocks) and
to ailouroeídhes sto kefáli (the feline on her head).

No, not that restaurant beside the Venetian *Arsenale*
employing exclusively waiters from
the mountain village of forgotten movie idols
men of stately quiffs and thoughtful mopeds –
Buscemi, De Niro, and somehow David Walliams.

Although it excels in many dishes, not least
the Chaniote *bouréki*, a courgette and *misíthra* pie
while its *arní sto foúrnou* and *kalamári*
(lamb from the oven and fried fresh squid)
are marvels of the long and slow and short and fierce.

But rather the oddly-angled field I see
each morning from my window in Broiniero,
a matt orange stretch of burnt August stubble
cleared amid a hillside of trees across the valley
which, if you look carefully, is in the shape of a ship

with the lane down through the trees its single mast,
and if it's not, try drinking in the middle of the day
then look again. This is how distinctly
the sirens could see Odysseus sailing by
upon the ocean-potion. If you look harder still

113

you can see a man wandering down the lane
with an oar, the 'wing of a ship', and a bee in each ear,
stings pointed outward. If you look
harderer stiller, you'll see inscribed upon
the left sting is *'oud'*, and on the right is *'eis'*.

He is looking for the wayfarer who Tiresias
has told him he will meet, who takes no salt
with his meat, who does not know a winnowing shovel
from a wooden helicopter rotor, who has blown here
like chaff. The wayfarer is you.

Karnagio: shipyard.

The Library of Bronze

variation on a theme by Orhan Pamuk

One night all the statues of Burns
came to life at the one unannointed moment.
There was a worldwide squeal of necks
in doubletake at where he found himself,
then down he stepped into small towns
so far from understanding
they hid in their houses as he clanked down
thin streets looking for a bar or garage
serving some kind of necessary oil
and wishing he had been equestrian.

Part-Talos, part tale-teller,
he habbied through fences and forests,
fording single oceans in a series of rhetorical leaps;
part-author, part-Terminator
he flyted unquaking Shakespeares
and clasped the hands of a legion of Pushkins
before congregating in the town of his birth,
all its flesh inhabitants having fled
beyond the toughened tourist fence
to sell tickets and telescopes.

And there the statues lived in promiscuity
with fridges and washing machines,
meeting nightly to compare
verses scratched on the bonnets
and in the windscreens of cars
cannibalised into their vast library,
each written in bronze's incomprehensible dialect –
undoubtedly addressed to you, his rusty fiere,
but, as they debated, could these all be by
the same awoken Bard?

Epimenides the Liar

They fashioned a tomb for thee, O holy and high one –
The Cretans, always liars, evil beasts, idle bellies!
But thou art not dead: thou livest and abidest forever,
For in thee we live and move and have our being.

MINOS, in the *Cretica* of Epimenides

Sleeper in the Dictaean Cave, which incubated
Zeus Cretagenes, you snorted through
fifty-seven years of dream dictation;
your skin His first page, its verse tattoos
changed you into the leopard of the Lord:
waking, you pronounced in paradox,
were walking prophecy, a naked book.

Mycenaeans, keen as foxes at the kill,
grinning Ithacans with homes to get through,
made their rank bed in Minoan rubble:
you raised into myth that which they barely knew
both they and fire and flood had razed –
since their minds were secondary, you erased
both truth and *technē* for the sake of Zeus.

You saw us with the muses' insect eyes:
slack appetites in sackfuls of forgetting flesh,
so made the Great Island, from maze
to mountaintop, the bedrock to all text,
alphabet in cleft and column; then set loose
a plague of sheep upon the Areopagus
to plant the shrine for your *Agnostos Theos.*

The Spartans thought your pelt could crack all codes
so hung it in their court in place of odes.

NOTE: For St Paul's use of Epimenides, see *Titus*: 1, 12; Acts: 17, 28.

The Bat

In dusk, from in among the walnut tree
and its bearing down upon the damaskina,
although we never see the bat unwrap
like a sticky sweet from the paper

of suddenly frictionless voiceless wings,
it begins to bi-, to trilocate, to be
anywhere at once in air's old film, wavering
with half-seen insects – it's in the field,

the garden, even underneath the canopy
of vineleaves that, by day, shades the little patio.
We watch the sky a dropping sun's turned gray
after an hour of lemon, mango, watermelon –

though this still lets some light be gleaned
through a wing like a sallow, puffed-out cheek,
a torch shone through a bloodless hand,
but gone in the second you understand

as though showing how exactly we must leave
each day – and do – a gathering of senses, sights
too small or intricate to count as insight,
too brief to form what we'd call belief.

The bat, that master of departures, is lost
to night, forgetting as it misses each leaf
and every branch: a figure of omnesia,
the way the world desires to be the past.

Paskha

At the fourth watch, the mountains exhale a moon
DU FU

1

Cold Crete, that paradox at *Paskha* – for us,
its usually summer guests, though every field
attempts to compensate us with its spume,
its fragrant wave of marguerites, we cluster in
our kitchen, cheap heater and our jumpers on
until Apostolos tells us it's time for church.

Made twice the *xenos* by this Britishness
of rain, I'm watching with a doubled eye
the televised delivery of the *phos* –
light from the Holy Sepulchre by plane –
it keeps, like August rolled in April's egg,
becoming the moon last summer in Mathes, born

as it appeared out of the mountain's flank,
a geodesic dome released from limestone –
Dafnokorfi in darkness, her lightbulb medusa.
Then as we leave I glance up at the globe
above our kitchen door and see inside it
a scorpion's corpse in silhouetted crux.

So all the way downhill to Broiniero
I'm troubled by the brain's chimeric quoins,
its both-at-onceness, how the memory's
assembled with our present self for parts,
as though the guy they'll burn upon the bonfire
turned out to be part-Judas and part-lobster.

2

The village cram into the glaring *eglisía*
divided into genders, bound into one stare –
the slaughterman's still-unshaven chin greets me
his wife gives Deb her swift, Maureen O'Hara smile –
a sharing out of tapered brown wax candles,
depositing of kisses on the icons' cheeks.

The bearded boys in black outside all know
it is important that the church be kept
surrounded by a firework halo, but not,
apparently, that they should wait till midnight –
all brightness is abruptly snuffed out by
a single hand, but while, behind the iconostasis,

everything inverts, divides, reverses, then,
connected to light's source, corrects, as though
seen through a keyhole into Heaven's offices –
out here the normal darkness sits inside us.
Our urgent crowding to the Babbas's new candle
looks like those old municipal mapboards where,

by pressing buttons for the library, the pool,
small bulbs would show you where to go – but all
you wanted was to press them all at once
and make the town light up to your small night:
now every man's a bright amenity,
and every woman's a well-lit hall, a park.

3

While everyone begins progressing out
and round, the icons high, the bonfire roaring,
the storyboard of the iconostasis starts
to shift beneath my dazzled gaze until
the risen Christ comes rushing up the escalator
from Hell (*Xristos anésti? Alithos anésti!*) –

but with His own, much-Veronicad features on
the scorpion's corpse, two labrys in His claws
and stinging every man upon his brow,
each woman in her womb, and with each axe
cleaving us open to the storehouses within,
the wordless libraries of viscera and skull

where under-languages are catalogued
by scholar tragelaphs, hippalektryon archivists:
what gryphons summarise in cuneiform
the minotaur confirms in Linear A,
the basilisk, an autodidact, glares
at centaur colts, while at her desk the Sphinx presides.

Home, cupping the candle flames like holding roses
by their heads – smudged above our threshold, a soot cross
beside the scorpion. First, entrail soup,
the pissy *margaritsa*, then sheep's lungs, wrapped
like giant cotton buds in more intestines –
gut instinct fed, and blankets on our beds.

Pilgrim Street

5 *Asterion*
(for Debbie)

To have no motive makes your route a maze:
the labyrinth of such passivity
will lead you to compose the hope one phrase
may cause the lucky murk to set you free
from that deep groove each second's self can't see
the minute hand of habit helps him dig –
one phrase the dream wrote down and crammed beneath
your pillow, there to morph from babe to pig:
the memory's half-prison and half-palace
where Dedalus becomes both Minotaur and Alice.

– There has to be a paean here to Crete,
a full-on Gravesian myth-kitty scratch
for that arch-backed Psipsinna isle, complete
with recipes for history's best batch
of stone *boureki*, guides for where to watch
Gort's father, Talus, first of robots, guard
the beaches like a bronze-browed Bandersnatch –
this is the ochre turf of Epidamnus, bard
of paradox – roll down the night-cab's pane:
wild thyme and fox piss say you're home from home again.

You'll find the Hotel Labyrinthos at
that neat illegal left into Georgioupouli
which everybody takes: first, greying flats,
its random, run-down stack of balconies,
and then tavernas, mini-marts, the sea;
and where the once-malarial Almirou
still meets the bay, great eucalyptus trees
give shade to tourists wondering what to do
with all this time they've bought. Let booze and food
and sun bewilder them to sleep: the myth holds good.

Though why should Theseus fail to register
beyond a walk-on on my storyboard
of psycho-machi-allegori-core?
Is it because he has the final sword?
What is the matter with this matador
that he's so unadored, unlike Lord Byron –
both man and beast enough that none were bored
should he drop anchor in their flesh environs?
The hero simplified to butcher brings
too little to an island stocked with gods for kings.

There's Zeus or Minos or Asterion –
throw Rhadamanthus in the royal mix
of demi-goddish fathers, bullish sons –
alive: part-Pharaoh and part-Pontifex;
dead: judges in stiff session past the Styx.
Achaean Theseus whacked them obsolete
the way time pressed the archaeopteryx
beneath the pounding strata of its feet –
Crete's strange chimeric Kings were overthrown
so ordinary monsters could ascend the throne.

And then there were the women: Pasiphaë,
they fancied, hid inside a wooden cow:
beware how Greeks revise your myths as lies –
all chthonic power tamed to porn's low brow.
Though Ariadne's thread, that one true tow,
revealed their trope of labyrinth was just
a ravelled palace – rhetoric unhoused,
Nietszche must write her how his wits were lost.
Then Gaia, giving birth, dug in her nails
creating Curetes to out-shout Zeus's wails.

Melisseus, whom Graves proclaimed a drone,
was bee-man boss of Cretan corybants –
those martial dancers Zorba would have known
but Zeus might just have got confused with ants:
Despots, or, *pace* Rob, Despinas, can't

distinguish loyal subjects from the herd –
or fear initiative in supplicants.
And Hebrew for Despina, queen of words
and bees, is Deborah – I might have known:
to serve the Goddess somehow's scrimshawed on my bone.

6 UNSCROLLED

Find us like archaeology –
we were here, we lived, and our story
is disorganised, unfinished. Here's our breath that scorched the Wall,
here are the sacred oracle stones
reduced to dust; here name, surname, when, how –
are emptied, and everything only sounds as though it could be
understood.

AMIR OR

We are born as though plucked from the mulberry bush
ripping open the silk.
we beat back the disgrace of our cheap cotton shrouds
and the arrogance of coffins.

NIDAA KHOURY

Viva Let!

I only ever tie a reef knot now
when I get on a beach and must remove
my deck-shoes, lash them to each other, then,
as horseless cowboys shoulder saddlebags,
I sling them, let my rolled-up trousers soak,
and freeze the interstices of my toes.

That's only twice this year: in Whitley Bay
today, among the Labradors that snap
at wave crests, slap-soled joggers, wet-skinned kids
about to kiddy-surf; and Tel Aviv
in May, when it is hot enough to tan,
but only crazy, night-flight trippers dip.

Jawbones of Bauhaus, buried in the sand
back in our orange-scented forties, and
stray dice of Deco, shaken on the groves
beside that shattered, unsheltering sea,
gave birth to Dizengoff's white spinal street,
the dentures of the Cinema Hotel.

Unspooling, we checked in beneath a screen
where Laurel spread his kilt across the puddle
Hardy fell right through into a glass
of outsized Guinness found by Frug Street like
a gyros, luring us towards the beach,
treating our needs like tugs upon a line.

As though emerging from the rusting pod
some sculptor's left upon the promenade,
we wandered Jaffa-ward between the strip
of giant stepped hotels, small hummus bars,
and regular deposits of fake reef,
resisting our first beerski till past ten.

St Mary's Lighthouse stands in for that port
that Rody marched towards as Glescae folk
did here pre package tours, while we sprawled at
a beach bar where the Rendezvous Café,
dead Julia's favourite, now stands. Just so
far things get laced to near, peace comes to grief.

And later, when our act was pulled together,
we drove past that mosque completely dwarfed
by a hotel's frame, to leave the spines of fish,
a baby-doting tax inspector, in
Aaron's ribachki restoran, strolled past
Armenian nunnery, Franciscan church,

and found the wishing bridge, not well, that wants
to cross, to tie luck to its only view,
that whitened hopeful city, Tel Aviv.
The rail is carved with zodiacal signs:
I stood before the crab's claws, let my thoughts
run sideways to our naming of those knots,

the reef and its untrusted opposite,
the matriarch-maligning granny; how
all rooted love must leave us, how mine could
not, at the end, let go, and how she did.
Each time I feel the gripless waves release
my ankles as I pace the shorelines' cord.

Touching the Wound

Why should we be allowed to go,
those too agnostic even to know
how in this grim divided age
to manage any pilgrimage,
far less approach the omphalos
of faith, its rock, its wall, its cross?

And yet I queue up with the good
to visit that Sepulchritude
segmented like a Christmas pud
so each church has its slice to brood
on beans and sixpences and rings:
its holy, holier, holiest things.

Armenian, Russian, Catholic –
the stone of unction cheek by cheek
both with Golgotha and the tomb –
a cosmos crammed into a room
where priests demark where women weep,
the Copts kept on the roof like sweeps.

The tomb is full, the faithful surge,
so I descend, past where they scourged,
down stairwells the crusaders scratched
as though a swarm of crosses hatched,
burst from these bowels of the rocks
to feast upon the Orthodox.

Because belief could choke this well,
the world was emptied to a shell
where places like Byzantium fell
because what was not here was Hell.
We queue to touch an emptiness
that means our suffering must be blessed.

I lie down at the chapel and
with Thomas's ignostic hand,
caress the symbol of His wound,
that axle-shaft worn in the ground,
a sheath of stone, a mould of rood,
that absence where it never stood.

Mid-Life Christ

Is frankly disappointed by the gnomes
or apostles as he hears they style themselves
these days of receding gums and shorelines
in their soft-boiled rewrites of his very grain.

He mooches, half-working in the shade,
keeps taking the finished board, the flawed saw
outside, to check them in the light
that turns everything to a species of limestone.

What's it going to take to persuade these people
that some things are meant to be a parable?
Must he drown upon a watery stroll,
rot upon a self-made cross?

He personally visited them all
after that last glorious rumour,
took Thomas to confirm there were no wounds
till he was blue in the ribs with proof.

And still they've spun it their several ways,
all the Jonah-come-latelies on a mission
to convert the light into a few believers
in that which they can only be and not believe.

Nothing spreads like the semblance of a truth.
Presumably Caesar would shut their mouths –
not that any fist puts out that Pentecostal glister
you get from never listening.

A lot of the old zeal has gone out of him these days,
like muscle tone or the falling water table.
He cycles a lot, just round the village,
just to keep in shape, really.

Says less and less, even to Adam
his deliberately illiterate son of a man.

Unscrolled

1 *The Highway*

A highway has been prepared for us:
we hurtle between the blank pages of desert;
between the empty mishnah of a mountain wall
and the wordless surah of a wadi, speed toward the Sea

a highway has been prepared for us

Between tin shack Bedouins wedged in a gorge, between
their wandered camels and the hilltops that blink
with whited settlements, salt of the latest villas,
a highway has been prepared for us

we speed toward the Toten Meer

Past the concrete block detention castle foursquare
at the junction to Jericho, where car-horns blare.
We fail to go to Bethlehem
for fear of never getting home

a highway has been prepared for us

At the garage cafe stop we watch three beefy men
in the children's playground going round
on a small cage-like roundabout, one of them
smoking to complete the experience

we speed toward the Sea

This is me unscrolling me
forgetting everything I'm told
forgetting how I came to here
forgetting I was ever old

2 *The Sea*

Here those who can
and those who cannot
wear a bikini

are equally buoyant.
Chocolate eared, lids lacquered
every feature a smear

here's Martin Sheen
and the blubber machine
formerly known as Bill:

Anthony and I appear
to have an evisceration
or baptism to attend.

here everything is taken
with a kilogram of salt, so
my whaleguts reach out, relaxed,

even though they know
the River Jordan
is on the other side.

This is me unscrolling me
forgetting everything I've done
forgetting I was ever cold
forgetting I'm my mother's son

3 *The Bad Son*

The bad son is floating in the dead sea
having committed seppuku of his sceptic intellect
hara-kiri of his unhealthy harns, he asks

When did I gain this spine of pumice,
this arse of polystyrene?

The bad son is test-driving his salty crucifix
having sat upon the waters of the dead, toes nibbled
by shoals of the shades of baccalau, he asks

Is this what it's like to manatee?
Do I dugong along? Am I Dead Sea-cowed?

The bad son rolls the water between his fingers
like money, the salt a palpable oil, but still rolls over
to ask the mud on the bottom of the sea

Now my lids are sealed with salt like a jar,
how shall they open to air again?

4 *The Mud's Reply*

Surely you know the flavour of your own eyeball?
The name of the djinn you've locked within?

This is the most the moist the post
after-coital après-postal double-jointed

past anointment missed appointment
practically post-corporeal but no

nowhere is the only place the dead can go
Aeneas didn't follow, nor

Odysseus talk his walk within,
nor will Orpheus sing his way out of that whole

this is the stink of disaffection
the ink that can't write 'resurrection'

let the rabbi Jesus wash your face
then open your eyes and think

I'm unscrolling till I am unscrolled
forgetting everything I've said
I'm unrolling my lids' blindfold
forgetting everything I've read

5 *Qumran*

We come to the baked-out mikvahs still unclean
the inkless scriptorium as yet unlettered
by remembering their rule
as barely as the earth
we are impure.

It looks as though the hills clawed out
lion grooves in the dust
and the zealots built around them
It feels like there is sand
in the very name.

We stare up at where goats know the caves to be
once pupilled with jars of dry papyrus:
our eyes are useless in this light –
too aqueous, their corners nibbed
with salt and sleep.

Here the air itself's a page
polished by the hard pebble of the sun
this blinding light the recto
and the frozen night
its verso.

Day writes itself over and over
in that white scalding ink
we can only read played out
in scarlet calligraphy on
the inside of the lid.

Particles of datable dust
blew into the lukewarm ink
as the scribe was writing:
the Torah blinked
but there they remain.

Forgetting what's living
forgetting who's dead
I am unscrolled
I return to wage peace on Jerusalem

Jerusalem Traveller

1

My little Socrates in Zion,
my gadfly in the Palestine
when did you decide to accompany me
clinging to my scalp by your able jaws?

Was it when I wove between
the settlers slung with carbines
and donned the pearly yarmulke
and approached the Wall?

Did you bite me then?

When I found my hand caressing the stone
wedged with wishes, scrolls and imprecations,
when the man stumbled up to us
rhapsodic in his welcome –

Did you bite me then
for the first and tender time?

I looked into his face, grizzle-bearded and glistening
as though we were reconciled to our strangeness
at home here in the strangeness of God
as though my travelling was done.

And all my prayers were stutters,
shreds of clauses threaded between
the intercostals of doubt:
did you bite me then?

2

Or was it when, turned away from the Bab-al-Qattanin
and turned away from the Shaar HaShalshelet
told to return day after day
by the same women and men at arms

I turned into an Arab barbers
all hair-flecked fingers and fly-blown movie stars
and amused companions calling from the street
as he stripped my skull to a Stan Laurel flap

Did you join me then?

When I gazed into a wall of glass like the open gate
to the Temple Mound as though I could climb
through my own silver-edged face
and onto that most serene of spaces –

Did you find me then
in that frame between the door-frames?

And when, searched and sent
up the archaeologists' rickety ramp
and loosed upon the plain of peace
to circle but not to enter the Dome

in the first space where my elbow
found room in the air, where my foot found its level
and the eye in my head found its bevel
and all Jerusalem below:

why did you bite me then?

Conviviencia

The writer's son picked us up on the road between the two hotels. One, the YMCA, was designed by the architect of the Empire State so that giant monkeys could admire its cool, foot-worn tiles and much-handled banisters and well-used reading-room when they picked it up by one of its three towers and shook it, then peered in though the windows. The other was the King David where John Major and Phil Collins had signed the floor along the longest corridor along with politicians like Netanyahu and Aznavour and the Gipper.

Although it was still warm and honeyed I could see the writer's son was following a wisp of darkness through the streets like the transparent speckled skin you wash off a squid or a turning trail of frogspawn in a pond. He had the aircon on full blast so that, when we caught up with the smoky end of the wisp, it was immediately caught in the radiator's robotic jaw and came poking out of the vents.

'Quick, tie it to something!' he told us.

We managed to get hold of the slippery dry stuff and knot it around the metal support for a head-rest, though it kept trying to untie itself. Then we hauled on it, looping it round and round the seat-backs like a cross between a scarf and a mooring line.

Soon we turned into a lane full of it, heading up out of the city onto a thin hill, as though night had fallen down this one side of a spur of street and none of the others. As more of the sooty, jelly-like darkness poured through the vents and even the cassette speakers, becoming obscurely audible as it did so, like a call to prayer, we could see the Settlements, behind the angular snake of their Wall, shining on promontories of evening sun.

The writer's house was down one of those lanes that, like smoke ascending into a clear sky, grow narrower and narrower, until only an emaciated donkey could hope to pass. His was the very last

138

house, a concrete-built, seventies-looking facade, with some older sections tumbling down the far side of the hill, but by the time we got out of the car, it was so completely dark I couldn't tell where these began or ended.

As the writer welcomed us, standing on the threshold of his home, I noticed the narrowest moon, the slightest sliver, sitting directly above him. I wondered which planet it normally orbited.

Son after son rushed to present us with dish after dish – roasted chicken, stuffed vegetables, cool salad – pouring squash from large plastic bottles into my grandmother's tumblers between the piles of neatly-folded dolmades and meaty kibbeh. Every now and then his wife, the silent author of this feast, would usher in another grandson, find him a seat at the ever-lengthening table, and, smiling at us and nodding, attempt to stuff him with food.

At this point, when I could no longer see the far end of the room, the writer began, at our insistence, to talk about his work.

Hezekiah's Tunnel

...the axes were against each other and while three cubits were left to
cut[?] ... the voice of a man...
called to his counterpart, (for) there was ZADA in the rock...'
SILOAM INSCRIPTION

Why should the kings of Assyria come, and find much water?
2 CHRONICLES 32: 4

Tunnelling is the simplest labyrinth
where we create direction blow by blow.
Two work-gangs hollowed loudness, chipped below
the city, hoped, between the outer spring
and inner pool, to meet – their labouring
could thus prolong a siege. Each couldn't know,
except by sweat-plugged ear, the other's clinks,
less clear than kings' grand plans, those nearing notes –
twin tocks to their swung ticks – which had to mean
a door could be unlocked: an exit from the dream
of rock into each other's eyes. Along the seams,
that song of stone linked Hezekiah's teams,
and judged them by the tunnel's kinks and torts.
Thanks to that *zada* – resonance – within
the rock, a blinded serpent route was cut,
which linked Siloam's thirst to Gihon's drink.
Sennacherib and his pack failed to outlive
the angel, plague or some domestic plot –
which leaves us with two gangs who in the gut
of darkness listen for each other's picks.

Pilgrim Street

6 *No Man*

Who'd be their mirror's image? Occasional,
alarming, mute – that's how we seem to most
of our acquaintance: why should they recall
what we pronounce, portentous as a ghost?
Our prophecies go missing in the post,
between the pillar box and lobby mat
of vague regard most scribblings get lost,
we are that backwards music heard by bats:
nobody's blues. Ear to the looking glass
you might just hear your reputation marching past.

Nobody and their looking glass shall see
nothingness doubled and redoubling till
the eye is shot into infinity,
a voyaging with neither wind nor sail,
still incomplete between breath and the will.
You fog the glass and see a mariner
or seem to, nearing through that curving veil,
old Zeno's leagues of instants: who you were
or who you will be, you can't tell – now, tell a lie:
why won't you look that apparition in the eye?

Because a nobody's a type of sin
now fame's our virtue, failures are consoled
present indifference means you'll one day win –
outside your lifetime's park, with different goals.
But that's obscurity's excuse for rules,
which liberates both players and the game:
no echo here of regs that hobble fools;
no chants, no crowds, no stadia, no names.
No skills are needed on a pitch so small
where everyone's a ref and no one has a ball.

But every poet is a nobody
to most of those who say they like to read
and mean the simple dead, plus two or three
the press explain are in the perfect lead
to be the era's metonyms in deed
and hopefully in print. Biography's
the apophenic art, which tries to weed
significance from chance – most hear its plea,
and few prefer that coiled complexity
the symbol spins out of a truth to set it free.

For nobody's that constant, clued-in reader
who understands why you keep leaving time;
who's nodding while you mash Krautrock with lieder,
or follows why you fossick other climes –
not seeking the exotic or sublime,
only directions for that journey home
you've never quite completed here, a mime
who cannot leave their abstract booth, glass tomb
in a cathedral to that martyred sense
Saint Sound, an absence granted by the audience.

Embrace all second places, spurn the spoils
gnawed on by the slow to comprehend
they're just another generation's foil,
winners who fail to grasp you jump off-trend
fast – slip beside the point or, best, behind,
before your self-importance gets impaled
upon the limitations of our time;
stay half-rhyme fluid – what you lose on sales,
credit or credibility, you gain
in heartsick wanderings and the hubris to abstain.

Between the divas and dogmatics, I –
or someone sounding just like me – must go
to Sofia or Jerusalem, and try
translating tunes which Dante didn't know;

to Tomsk, Kashgar, Hargeisa, as the flow
decides – Caracas for the western arm:
fish out Khant ballads from beneath the snow,
hear Amanissa Hanim's Twelve Muqams,
a herder's *hees* in the airstrip's quickened dusk,
the song of *el caballo viejo*, thick with musk.

7 SOMALILALIA

The country teems with 'poets, poetasters, poetitoes, poetaccios': every man has his recognised position in literature as accurately defined as though he had been reviewed in a century of magazines – the fine ear of this people causing them to take the greatest pleasure in harmonious sounds and poetical expressions, whereas a false quantity or a prosaic phrase excite their violent indignation.

RICHARD BURTON, *First Footsteps in East Africa*

Flying Backwards

'Where are *you* going?' swaggered the stick,
rapped lightly against arriving ribs
till a wave from a journalist – my FT pal –
already sat at the bungalow for VIPs,
got me off the runway for some sweet red tea.

'Where are you *going?*' jollied a jellaba
back on Djibouti's runway in our brave twin-prop –
half-pencil case, half-Lada. Outside,
the seats were being removed from its comrade
so sheep could board, then promenade.

'Hargeisa, insha'Allah' prayed its pilot
and a glance behind caught the engineer a-
kimbo on our luggage with a shaky thumbs up.
An hour of glassy scrub, then two rocky cones:
'See there? – the titties of Hargeisa!'

'Where *are* you going?' the hijab had hummed
on the flight out from Heathrow, a tiny mother
perched upon a bale of cloth for others –
and when the answer widened those eyes:
'Are you a journalist?' – I had no reply.

She could, by a dextrous twist upon
the necessary hour, pray in her seat
while I anticipated everybody's question
as though my insides knew.
Where was she heading? 'Home to Mogadishu.'

'*Where* are you going?' tasked a telephone,
its actuary eagerness to sell upon
the wane, then told my ear the same
re a former colony as the FO:
'Somaliland? – No coverage for there.'

News from Hargeisa

Somali Bedouins have a passion for knowing how the world wags...
news flies through the country. Among the wild Gudabirsi the Russian
war was a topic of interest, and at Harar I heard of a violent storm,
which had damaged the shipping in Bombay Harbour, but a few weeks
after the event.

RICHARD BURTON, First Footsteps in East Africa

1

First thing: a simcard from the tower of TeleSom,
that meant – anywhere – I could call home,
including the desert's heart, Laas Geel,
where my mother called to ask if I was ill (I was).

No: first first thing, Gaarriye in a 4x4
straight through security – papers and chains a bore –
the poem's a Somali open sesame; then home
past grand hotels, slabbed off from car-bombs

that never came; qat booths and the dry-throat river;
past shops named after him – purveyors
of electronics, fridges; the Brit-built parliament,
decayed and delaying; the new Obama Restaurant.

We sped through everything, punctual as news or qat
itself, to a little backyard, its allotted slot of stars.

2

Beneath his lime-green eaves in the white-tiled strip
of courtyard, carpeted to make a bedroom,
I stare at the stars as Gaarriye points out Gurey
like a square sky-robot, tiny-headed hero,
doomed offspring of a murderous she-djinn –
his only choice was matricide. Is this how to begin
in Hargeisa – my hotel room unslept-in,
frozen in the comet-tails of conversation,
stories for the lines that link the stars?

Between soft pancake mornings of fresh papaya, clove tea,
and smoky kitchen evenings of Somali classes,
(*kuluyl* is heat and *qiiq* is smoke), the grammar of samosas
(*macaan* is delicious); the night sky become a visor
through which the Moon stares down on our sleeping faces –
we begin to live inside air's letterbox, outside
the women's way with folding, wiping, frying, words,
that lifts the children through their courtyard years:
stories as the lines that link their stars.

3

The hyena and the lion shared a kill
and the lion, as befits a king, said, 'Split
the carcass and the innards and the bones
between us so we both may dine.'
The hyena gave the lion nine-tenths
of the poor gazelle and grabbed the rest –
his king roared out, 'What's this?' and raked
the creature with its claw-stuck club
of a paw so hard an eyeball hung
like white fruit on the smirker's cheek.

A fox came trotting from the darkness:
'Let me see the portion that he took –
why, you should have nine-tenths of this!'
and so divided it, and then, before
the lion spoke, said, 'Still, a king must have
nine-tenths of what remains...' and so,
though it was only cartilage and gut,
divided it once more, and then again,
until the lion had its share, and let
the fox and all his kinsmen live.

4

Gaarriye checking Al-Jazeera daily for the latest
in the hot curtain-drawn long low-sofa sitting room
re the US captain bobbing in his Hitchcock lifeboat
off Puntland with three doomed pirates

149

did they but know it, while I note down parables
and chafe to see the MiG parked by Gobannimo Market
where Siyaad Barre strafed his own citizens
and we buy mp3s of oud music, ounces of frankincense –

which Mas'ūdī mentions in *The Meadows of Gold*
as the whole coast's only ancient export – *kundur*,
great scoops of its heady grey gum for a few wads
of shillings; swathes of *shammaad*, women's cloth,

patterns like shadows scissoring bougainvillea,
for which Gaarriye reckons he can get me a deal.
Back home past exposed cellars and piled breezeblocks:
a massive new build they simply call 'MI6'.

5

There is a tree upon the moon
a sparse old country much like ours
whose each leaf mirrors one of us
and when we're born it's glad and green
and as we grow it burns to gold
and when we sicken it turns white
and when we're dying then it drops
falling for forty days and nights
and no one knows which is the cause
and which is the effect, but when
it touches for the first time here
and curls up, as it dries we die.

6

We slept so close
to the silent pool of sky
that when the baby cried
it was as though the moon
wept papaya-coloured light

as though it could believe
the galaxies infect us with music

150

like Gaarriye's toothache groans,
till all our infant languages
learn to praise the night

so while we slept
and the blue dogs curled in the road
Hargeisa's dry stars knelt
and kissed our brows
with insects for their lips.

At the Crossroad

In the calligraphy of broken roads we read
the fork for Boorama or Ethiopia: down the latter
the qat-trucks hurtle every rattling morning

past battle-sites and through *barwaaqo* –
God-spots where the rain collects – so punctual
that young leaves reach each opening mouth.

The former takes us to Amoud, that university
where the prosody of *maanso* and *hees* propounds
Somaliland as a single alliterating sound.

At Kalabaydh the crossroad's options say
I'm looking at a nation down these double needs:
the leaf it needn't yet distinguish from

the voice which drew me here, despite the world –
'There is no war because the people do not will it.'
But back in Gabiley, all the road announces is

an avenue of trees, each standing for a marriage,
all reach a certain height at which, agreed,
they spread their canopies out, and rest.

The man who's kitted out his wheelchair
with hand-pedals speeds by where our convoy's paused,
the toothbrush in his breast pocket still in its packet.

The woman holds up a handful of citruses, so small,
green and fresh I can't tell if they're lemon or lime,
the way I don't know whether the herds are

as precisely sheep or goats as the line between
their black satin heads and cotton-clung bodies.
In the evening the couples come and compare their trees.

The Captives

Termite mounds step closer when your head turns,
towers that seem the opposite of edifice –
not constructed from below but as though
remains of some eroded solid, anterior to air,
the megalopolis that once gripped us all –

the way that Bete Giyorgis, that church in Lalibela,
sits within the pit, as though it dreamed itself
while still inside the rock they carved it from;
or Pompeii's smothered souls had found their feet,
zombie husks, shufflers by the roadsides,

frozen when you look, both fecal and phallic,
still enshrouded in sackcloth, still bonded –
a burqa of earth obscures their nearly faces,
they haul and lean in exhaustion, herd the unseen,
cloud shadows hint at their caprines, *riyo* or *ido*

ready to scatter in this rainy season; but
they pause, burdened by the cities within them
in a cityless place, their nerve tunnels, legions
of blind thoughts grubbing away, irrigating breath
through breathlessness, they anxiously approach

as though they have requests, questions about
release, curiosities that we could feed
but when we turn they will not speak,
these captives wandered far from some tomb
they should have been immured within,

from the rock that would have folded them
in its embrace, its chain that fused, the mouths
that should have been inscribed, the hand
that could have held, the chisel dropped away
and all the termite text escaping into earth

Riyo: goats; *ido:* sheep.

Hotel Rays

1

Hospitium enclosus: a wiry light cloisonnés the lawn
upon which, ambassador of grass, the tortoise lives –
slow lawnmower, cracked and shifting whaleback
in its square Sargasso, solemn gazer on
the kudu, streak-flanked as though it had just leaned
against a freshly-painted zebra. Neither may leave.

We breakfasted on liver and mango,
hardly mentioning the aid worker, shot
four years ago, but got the shivers when,
Gaarriye-less, the guard would not let us past
to climb a hillside that wanted to be a lane
through children playing, free as feathers.

2

After we'd read to the usual three hundred
in a hall for half that in the old boarding school
they'd declared Amoud University – plus a stunned row
of just-arrived Americans, tutors: suncreamed, headscarfed
and wholly unready for 'the fine ear of these people' –

Riyaale, wry Dean of Student Affairs, drove us up
to Old Amoud: a slave station en route to the Red Sea;
a territory he described as 'God's land', meaning
no one wanted to live there. Startling what must be
Phillip's dik-diks, darting from our flanks, we rose to rubble.

The city wall straggled at two courses; then strewn pottery,
pure quartz, sockets of fire-blackened millet stores –
sucking out the air with flame will keep the grain
for twenty years – just twenty years before he'd seen
walls up to the window-frames and the old chains.

'Brokers,' he said, looking down at Boorama's bowl
where colonials had hunted lion. 'We were brokers.'
We went back by a half-built hospital, stairwell
blocked with Saudi carpets. Broken, still mirrored
in a name, memory negotiates the cure or the kill.

3

The hotel's name, Rays, means the lying of fresh rain
on the ground, so, while yellow weaver birds,
possibly Speke's, plait their lunch-song
(*chinkichi-chewchew-skerinkitistew*),

and Martin and I discuss how in a poem
a conversation between a lover and a crow
can be like a camel with a peg through its nose
so it can't smell the calf it feeds,

suddenly, gently, then with great, dark-
spotted insistence, it begins to rain,
so fresh a smell it is as though
the air is being rinsed clean of song.

4

Before dusk could lean on the whole continent
another of Amoud's thirty-year-old Deans,
Axmed, took us out to the airport, to watch a herd
of goats taxi down its long dust runway,
and Martin persuaded the herder to sing a *hees*.

She giggled at our desire to hear goat-music as
the sun took off, and her black and white charges
turned grey as she swished sticks and sang to them
and the stone-curlews, the one flightless transporter
and the broad valley, asphalt-free to its hills.

Some boys were summoned by her song
arriving like the Constellation of the Haggler
to establish a rate for this. Axmed's advice –
nothing so generous as to cause
dispute between cousins over a voice.

5

And then the cry comes up and the cry comes up
from another and the cry comes up from
another and another mosque

the comfort of the calls to prayer
itself a kind of reply as they arise
almost at the same moment

on all sides around the little hilltop
of Buurta Sheekh Cali, up from the dark
and into the not yet dark

as though the delay was caused by darkness
itself, gathering around our prayers
as the kids play on the timbers stacked

below the mobile phone mast and the Sufi shrine
and pose for photos as this hill's last mosque sings out
a few lights are lit and the smell of woodsmoke rises

and as two girls run down the almost sheer slope in
their flip-flops and a mother in her patchwork hut
calls suddenly for flour and before

we descend to buy batteries and *caday*,
new bundles of toothbrush twigs on a streetcorner,
the cries continue ascending into the darker still,

rising to where everything is
still, where prayer will only consent to be heard
beyond the human ear

Saxansaxo (Driving Westward)

And being by others hurried every day,
Scarce in a year their natural form obey...
DONNE

Hours after the professoriate
have packed their cases, having chewed their qat,
it's time to be trying to race the rain
westward and home to Hargeisa.

Past the burnt-out tanks by Bad Luck Farm,
beside the tarmac if the track goes faster
like the arrowing swift, the *baaqfallaar*,
the driver keeps a nostril to the onrushing cloud.

We chafe at hamlets with a chain across
shell-pocked asphalt, guard-sheds from which
men amble to slap the poet's happy hand
and shout hello to us, *xerta* of alliteration's sheekh.

A Y-shaped treestump burns in the darkened
rain-stalked desert. When Gaarriye flings
a qat branch from the window it flies back
and slaps his brow like angry laurels.

Now even I inhale it, where the hills
are scoured back to a few scant pyramids,
between grit-blown trees that graft beside
the sere and sandy riverbeds: *saxansaxo,*

sweet scent of approaching rain
that means split wrist-bone beds of sunken rivers
will spate with an express engineered from water
and we must crowd at their crossings for hours.

As we hurry, half-reluctant, before rain's arrival,
I stare into a dream of streaming carriages
passengers nose-deep in the pulse of news:
Mas'ūdī and Burton, the imam John Donne.

157

Clockwork Fever

I'm ill while the rain lasts, scribbling in the little room
as a smart fusillade is maintained upon the metal roof
for merciless hours under the deeper artillery
of ceaseless thunder. Still, I doze through the *azan*:

see dozens of mullahs arise on the springs of wristwatches;
one insisting his clock is right, even though
he always starts later than his neighbours – don't I know
his plump cheeks, straight beard, half-spectacles?

His lips unconsciously purse as he checks the time,
as the slow spring uncoils beneath his feet
carrying him further into the crashing darkness...
Then it's cloudless, hot: everyone is post-nap, up

and shoveling the brook-bed of pools back into a lane.
A herd of goats wander up the street: between
their two rows of blank walls and metal gates
painted pale blue and set with wrought-iron hearts.

One kid rises on its hind legs to nut another, whereupon
four rush together to make companionable lightning.
A girl from London asks me how I like the food
and refuses to believe my reply.

Laas Geel

(a found poem)

Many anthropomorphs are painted on the walls
however they are less numerous than the bovines.
The thorax is wide and dressed with a kind of 'shirt'
sometimes drawn with vertical painted stripes.

The lower limbs are spindle-shaped, merged or
separated by a simple stroke or vertical space.
The upper limbs are filiform and always spread open
making the body appear cross-shaped. The head is small

either punctiform, rounded, or put on its side
and set above a truncated neck on which
are sometimes painted horizontal strokes
which appear like neck rings one on top of the other.

This head can be surrounded by a pointed 'crown'
or by small radiant dashes. In some cases a kind
of feather headdress appears on one side of the top of the head.
These characters sometimes carry a bow, a stick,

or possibly a small shield. They are systematically associated
with the bovines and are placed either under the neck
under the belly or more seldom behind the rump.
Besides the fact that they are sometimes with canids.

Berbera

But I was telling how I was inspired to visit Cilmi's grave,
To offer my homage, my salutations and my song...
    HADRAAWI

What lasts and what do we want to last
if memory's made new by thinking it again,
a fable finding its latest mouth each time
and lost beyond your final thought? Not

the drive to Berbera – a race with freshness,
since the day's catch would not be served
a moment later than, like everything Somali,
its optimum. So we blurred past the site

where a friend of Martin's father won his VC,
holding a hill with a handful of men
like the veterans we'd met at the NGO, still in
their scoutish uniforms, hair red with henna.

They stopped the Italian advance across
a border now as invisible to all
former and would-be future masters as
those medalled men, or this self-declared

republic, still fitting within its limits.
We dropped from the hills into coastal heat
like an undercarriage skidding on the runway
ahead, the only one long enough, they say,

to land the Shuttle outside of Houston. Not
the good smell, *udgoon*, of fried fish, *kalluun*,
in the salt and dusty haze past noon and by the Gulf,
tray-fulls in the guestless hotel, malt non-beer.

Not the swim, each breaker lifting its swirl of sand
into sunlight, the guards, lounging on cardboard,
no older than those boys who rushed into the surf
to help the diver drag his boat ashore – a Brit,

head filled with brilliant fingers of unbroken coral,
the unrecorded paths of migrating whales:
I was the nearest he could find to a tourist
so got to hear his perfect pitch.

Not the drive back into dusk and doubt,
talk of walking in the green pastures, *doog*,
as we reached white sand, mountains streaked
with black lava: *guban* and darkness where

I keep seeing lightning across the bush
no one else notices – rain somewhere other,
light's brief inhabiting of air, a striplight
attached to the flat cloud-ceiling that flickers.

Not that, neither our coming nor going,
but the search for the baker's grave,
Cilmi Bowndheri, who Hadraawi greeted
as his 'king among poets', Hodon's lover.

We found only a broken length, nameless,
collapsing back into powdery dirt,
no cemetery wall, no limit to its fading,
no end to the final act of his forgetting.

The Lamb

I hadn't been aware, although I'd watch
as his friends made that flicking gesture
at their throats, of the steady approach
of the liver for our final feast, borne
within the black-headed sheep
like a Sheban queen within her litter,

a Berbera blackhead selected by
Gaarriye's half-brother out past Gebiley
and driven here since our arrival
by steady switchings with his crook
like a Neapolitan's stroking of his cheek
sketching the scar of the hard man

I was not: some bug had stopped me
as though in the whole herd's tracks
so I missed reading with Hadraawi
in a hall I wandered later, looking through
the hot absence of seven hundred people
for a poem blown beneath the chairs

by the poets' breath – still shaky, with
no appetite, as though I were the paper.
So when a neighbour, in whose yard
the sheep had spent its first enclosured night,
handed me her well-honed, hair-thin knife
I couldn't amount to the honour,

and she, practical and brief, cut through
its butter neck where black head becomes
white throat, as though God's guidance,
almost severing it with that stroke,
and sent arterial plumes to pelt the wall,
and felled it in the little courtyard.

Gaarriye's youngest daughter laughed to see
its silly fall, but wept as lid and container
of those few years of grazing and sun's grace
continued to think they could be alive
as though there were some catch, some pin
that thrashing would rebutton up.

And then, instead of life, its echo:
the pipes within it sounding out their last,
and like an offering to summon ghosts,
the deep bowl blood made for itself
by gouging into dust, as the carcass
was seized and hung upon the porch.

And then I saw how the flies were gathered
like a shadow thrown into the air
by the sharp unlacing of the stomach wall,
presence of the viscera another visitor
as the liver, like a newborn lamb, was lifted
and we gathered for the feast.

Pilgrim Street

7 *Daedalics*

We're filled, the muses claim, with tripes and tropes –
among their ticks and scrawny-throated herds,
they perch upon their high, pine-stubbled slopes
and don't know how to tell us we diverge:
our bags of guts and bowls of words each surge
in contrary directions. Poor old flesh –
muscle, corpuscle, nerve – can only lurch
to burial, while neuron will enmesh
with neuron, till our consciousness constructs
a mind, which burrows birth-wards, claiming to induct.

Paideuma – that tangling of the roots by which,
Frobenius whispered in Pound's Greekish ear,
we apprehend how children of the rich
think they own history. Not that he could hear
for looking like a Sinologic seer,
nor could he see through Fenellosa's flaw:
the Chinese do not read the pictures, dear.
Confusion cooked his book and called it raw.
And parataxis is not ideogrammic,
unless it's truth with which you're being economic.

But every Dedalus forgets in turn
his home key through the practice of his art,
departs from Fibonacci when he learns
the goal was only useful as a start:
to build the labyrinth he must lose heart,
lose head, lose compass, hand and face –
let instinct tear his faculties apart:
the Minotaur can't know it's in a maze –
one whisper and his true creation's lost.
And so he haunts his life as though half-beast, half-ghost.

At forty-nine, Dunce Scotus Gyrovagus,
why still attempt books doubled as the labrys,
too troubled to read half of, thrown away as
OCD-meets-whim? Formally too barbarous
to draw the scholars to their proper libraries;
too full of hohos for the hoitytoit –
no one eternal note with candelabras;
too shirty and too shouty, too 'not quite' –
no hero, then, no Theseus, no Childe,
some porter gone to seed, his Walls of Troy grown wild.

Why did you, Dustie-Fute, compose in Scots –
a language no one's taught they need to read,
that's filled with forty synonyms for snot
and spoken mainly by the rural deid?
Our word for 'language', laughably, is 'leid' –
that's less the vanguard, more the zeppelin
which plummets from the 'lift' *qua* 'sky'. Who needs
to learn another English for their sins?
How many angels would it take, if Lallans
could skriek, or jist creh oot their names, to shift this balance?

What drove you to translate the lesser-known
rest of the world – Chinese, Somali, Turkish,
Bulgarian and Farsi? Chance alone,
or (this rhyme only works upon the ticklish)
some instinct that you must become unRilkeish?
Beyond the Eurodome it's audible
how Byron found a global sort of Unglish
that tells an angel from the ego's yell,
finds muses up muezzins, orreries
in Mandarin, and in Cyrillic how to sneeze.

And how on earth or on the moon to finish
this travelogue of the unravelling voice
which can't go home again? Say we just vanish
in a Cortina – neither Rolls nor Royce
would understand the weird behind that choice –

let's go. The essence is an excellence
at running, said auld Dedalus as Joyce:
beyond the gut-mind and the roar of sense
in Hotel Labyrinthos monsters greet:
the Silk Road and the Low Road meet on Pilgrim Street.

Omnesia

I left my bunnet on a train
Glenmorangie upon the plane,
I dropped my notebook down a drain;
I failed to try or to explain,
I lost my gang but kept your chain –
say, shall these summers come again,
    Omnesia?
You'd like to think it's God that sees ya
(while He's painting the parrots of Polynesia)
give your wife that fragrant freesia
   and not the eye of Blind Omnesia.

I scrabbled here and scribbled there –
a sphere of peers declined to care;
I roomed with hibernating bears
and roamed where cartoon beagles dare:
protect me by not being there,
Our Lady of Congealed Despair,
    Omnesia!
You'd like the universe to please ya,
your admin duties to be easier,
instead you grip the pole that's greasier –
   the shinbone of unskinned Omnesia.

I wibbled there and wobbled here,
forgot the thousandth name of beer;
I filled my head with clashing gears
and tried to live in other years;
I passed on fame, selected fear,
watered your name with 'Poor Bill' tears,
    Omnesia...
So you lack ambition and pelf don't tease ya?
still me-memed mugwump prats police ya,
and Brit-farce forces queue to seize ya
   for the purloined pearls of Aunt Omnesia.

I'd like to think the Muse remembers –
not that teaching starts in late September –
but the first of fire's dying embers,
that glow on Cleopatra's members;
my further lovers' choric timbres…
Did I fiddle with their numbers,
                    Omnesia?
You hope it isn't Fate who knees ya,
the Ship of Fools which makes you queasier,
or Mister Scythey come to ease ya
                    into the arms of Dame Omnesia.

ACKNOWLEDGEMENTS

'The Messages' was commissioned by the sculptor David Annand to be inscribed on a piece, 'Cubes', for Tesco's in Dundee. 'The Silver Bridie' appeared on *North Carr Light*. 'Rabbie, Rabbie, Burning Bright' and 'Cock of the North' appeared in *New Poems Chiefly in the Scottish Dialect*, ed. Robert Crawford (Polygon, 2009). 'End-Sang' was commissioned for *Headshook*, ed. Stuart Kelly (Hachette Scotland, 2009). 'An Epistle' was commissioned for *Addressing the Bard*, ed. Douglas Gifford (Scottish Poetry Library, 2009). The sequence *Muqam* appeared on *Mad Hatters Review*. 'Thersites', the sequence *A Myth of Scotland*, and 'Epode' were variously commissioned by BBC Radios 3 and 4. 'The Whale Road' was a collaboration with the artist Christine Kelegher for *Hidden Door*. 'The Library of Bronze' appeared in *Split Screen* (Red Squirrel Press, 2012).

Poems also appeared in *Almost Island, And Other Poems, Blackbox Manifold, Chapman, Edinburgh Review, Gift, The Guardian, Ink Sweat and Tears, Magma, Poetry International Web, Poetry London, Poetry Scotland, Poetry Wales, The Warwick Review* and *The White Review*.

I would like to thank the British Council, Cove Park, and the organisers of the Pamirs, Guangzhou, Poeteka, Venezuelan World Poetry and Druskininkai Festivals, for the stimulus behind many of these poems. Thanks also to Martin Orwin for his help and kindness re all matters Somali. I would also like to thank Linda Anderson and Jenny Richards, and my colleagues at the School of English Literature Language and Linguistics, Newcastle University, for all their support during the composition and completion of *Omnesia*.